*R*enaissance,

NOT Retirement

*For Men Who Have Enough Money
But Not Enough Life*

*R*enaissance, NOT Retirement

*For Men Who Have Enough Money
But Not Enough Life*

Robert E. Linneman, Ph.D.

Llumina Press
TAMARAC, FLORIDA

ISBN: 1-932560-73-4
Printed in the United States of America by Llumina Press

TO MY FATHER

Contents

STEP 4

The Paths

Explore Alternative Ways to Your Renaissance

Explore paths that seem right for you. Read case histories of people whose socioeconomic and demographic backgrounds are similar to yours. Then select a path to your own new beginning.

STEP 5

The Plan

Make Your Renaissance a Reality

Make the most of your most valuable resource—time. Follow an easy-to-use method for charting, following, and, when necessary, altering your course. Start enjoying a more fulfilling, enthusiastic, and energetic life—today.

STEP 6

The Communication

Give Your Renaissance the Standing It Deserves

A rose by any other name doesn't smell the same. The way you present your renaissance will govern the way it's perceived. Six suggestions show how to put your renaissance in the most favorable light.

Epilogue

A renaissance is not like winning the big prize one time only—it's a continual rebirth, always replacing the old with the new.

Acknowledgments

Although it was decades ago—a time when one's despair was not muted by Prozac, Paxil, Zoloft, or whatever—I can still hear my father's footsteps, sometimes at four o'clock in the morning, pacing back and forth in the upstairs hallway that separated our bedrooms. And I hear him pleading, "For God's sake, help me! What am I to do? Won't somebody help me?"

We wanted to. But we didn't have the answer.

A heart attack had forced him to retire at a fairly young age. He was fortunate in being financially secure. Although not rich, he owned his home, some land, some bonds, a few stocks.

But he was extremely unfortunate in another way. His work had been his life. He had few outside interests. Oh, in retirement he served as a board member of our church, he became a 32nd-Degree Mason, he looked after his investments, and from time to time we went on vacations. We tried to encourage him to expand these activities—and to find new ones. But nothing would fill the deep chasm left by the loss of his career.

He had enough money, but not enough life.

I loved my father. I believe my father's difficulty in retirement was the seed that germinated into this book. Although the findings are too late to help my father, they have already helped others, and they have also helped me. But how I wish I had known then—when my father was alive—what I know now. I believe I could have made a difference.

Working on this book has been one of the best experiences of my life. I interviewed literally hundreds of people, and virtually everyone I asked was eager to help. Some of the interviews were formal, some informal. Some lasted for just a few minutes, some for hours. I'll always be grateful to these people who were so willing to share with me—and through this book, others—their thoughts and experiences.

Published sources also provided perspectives and several case histories. Although references are cited in the Notes section, I'd like to single out a few: Gail Sheehy, *New Passages: Mapping Your Life Across Time* and *Understanding Men's Passages;* Vern Drilling, *Closing Doors, Opening Worlds;* Richard Bolles, *What Color is Your Parachute;* and the Web site 2young2retire. com.

All persons in this book are described as they were at the time of the interviews or the dates of the published sources, even though their situations may have since changed. Only the first names and the initial letters of the last names are given. In some instances I have changed the names and initials when even this partial disclosure might cause embarrassment.

I've been fortunate to have friends who listened patiently to my endless banter and reviewed rough drafts. Many of their suggestions have been incorporated in this book. Special thanks go to Ken and Phyllis Haldeman, Pat and Kathy Kirschling, Harold and Christina Klein, Charles and Suzy Patrick, Larry Poli, Jack Ritchie, John Stanton, and Sheldon Salaznick.

Lloyd DeBoer, a mentor and my doctoral thesis advisor from many years ago, has been a constant support, both emotionally and editorially. And Abdul and Blamah Sarnor have been great cheerleaders.

I must give high praise to the masterful developmental and editorial help from Doug Gordon and to the assistance from Doris Braendel, Laurel Marshfield, my brother, Bill, and my son, Dan.

But most of all, I'm indebted to my wife, Annabelle. Speaking of "endless banter," she heard the same stories over and over again as I related them to friends and acquaintances. And through it all, she's borne up well. Besides being so tolerant, she read through draft after draft of the manuscript, and time and again made most valuable developmental and editorial suggestions. Thanks, Annabelle.

Robert E. Linneman, Ph.D.
Valley Forge, PA

Renaissance,

NOT Retirement

For Men Who Have Enough Money
But Not Enough Life

Introduction

Ask Fred M., now in his 70s, how he feels. He'll tell you, "Excited! Happy! Fulfilled!"

Is Fred retired?

Well . . .

Fred did retire from his job as head of an automotive parts trucking company some years ago, but he had to spend several years finding out that retirement wasn't for him.

Fred had lots going for him. Stature in the community. Good family life. No financial worries. No more job responsibilities.

The first thing he did when he retired was hit the golf course—some weeks, almost daily. He studied travel brochures and took off on leisurely vacations with family and friends. He pulled out all the books he had intended to read "some day" and bought more. He liked woodworking, so he got some great new equipment. Why not try fishing? He bought a top-of-the-line bass boat.

Everybody's dream? Maybe. But Fred found himself feeling useless and miserable. "I did all those things you think you want to do—only to find out they weren't satisfying. I started drinking heavily and became an alcoholic.

"My family helped me through this period and I got some much-needed therapy. I came to the conclusion that I had been spending my time doing things that just weren't going to cut it."

Fred reached out in different directions. A friend was doing volunteer work for the Service Corps of Retired Executives (SCORE), and Fred was intrigued enough to try it himself. Through SCORE, Fred is able to use his skills and his decades of experience to help small businesses develop strategic and financial plans, learn better ways to market their products, streamline their operations, and find creative ways to fund their operations.

And how has SCORE helped Fred?

"I don't think I could ever adequately express my feelings, but there's such a satisfaction that I get from helping small business-people overcome their problems. SCORE also gives me the chance to stay up to date with current business methods and procedures, and that by itself is very worthwhile. Then, for me, the comradeship I have with other SCORE volunteer counselors is very important."

Today Fred spends 20, sometimes 30, hours a week as a regional director for that organization. He still has time for golf, traveling, reading, woodworking, and fishing. But his work with SCORE gives him a central purpose and meaning that his recreation activities, by themselves, didn't provide.

That's what Fred discovered.

He found his path to a new beginning—a renaissance, not retirement.

You, like Fred, can turn your retirement into a renewal, a rebirth of enthusiasm and commitment. But there's a good chance that you, also like Fred, won't get there by following the "storybook" retirement path of other retirees you've heard about.

If you've already given a lot of thought to retirement—and you're troubled by what you see—your worries may be right on the mark. In one study of retirees, 41 percent of the respondents found the transition from a career to retirement difficult. The adjustment was even more troublesome for those who measured their self-esteem by their careers.

Would you be one of the 41 percent?

For myself, if I would retire, I'd be among the troubled—for sure. My life has always been centered on my careers. I abhor the thought of retirement. I'm not nearly as afraid of death as

I am of obsolescence—of living a life without a compelling purpose for my existence.

The Myths of Retirement

In theory, retirement does seem attractive.

When you retire, you'll finally be free from the daily drudgery of your job or profession: free from endless bureaucratic meetings organized by drones, who (true to their name) buzz on with little purpose other than self-advancement.

Free from the daily toil of digesting reports, reading and writing letters and memos, listening to interminable phone calls.

Free from the stress of supervising unreliable, indifferent, and sometimes intractable employees.

Free from the hours lost in airport lines and lounges, and from eating dinners indistinguishable from their plastic containers.

Little wonder that while your car sat jammed in the nightly 5 P.M. traffic, wedged between two immovable objects on wheels, you dreamed of nonstop golfing, fishing, reading, traveling. Life on an idyllic beach, in a mountain fastness, in a gated retirement community.

Those dreams are natural for all of us. Yet you sense there's something wrong with those scenarios.

The Realities of Retirement

Even if you've always longed for more time to play golf, fish, or pursue other hobbies, you may wonder if these activities will be enough. Or, you may have already tried retirement and found that it's not the fantasy life it's often cracked up to be.

Think for a moment about how you'll feel in retirement. At first you may sigh with relief: "This is what I've worked for, isn't it?" After a while, though, the novelty will wear off, and you'll "settle" into retirement.

As your new role emerges, you'll likely experience a number of unpleasant changes. Some may be subtle as the touch of a feather, and others may hit you like a hammer.

Overall, you may not like what's happening during your retirement days.

Let's examine five of the less-than-desirable metamorphoses that often occur in retirement.

Reality #1: You May Lack a Sense of Accomplishment

Our jobs provide prestige, power, control, and satisfaction. Among life's activities, many of us receive the greatest sense of achievement from our jobs. We thrive on meeting important challenges, receiving public acknowledgment of our successes, feeling like we're a part of a purpose that is larger than ourselves.

All that changes with the typical retirement.

And if you believe, like many retirees, that you're not accomplishing anything worthwhile, thoughts of obsolescence and uselessness will become your constant companions. Oh, on some days you may feel healthy, vibrant, and ready to take on the world, but on others you'll feel so depressed you'll wonder if it's worth your effort to drag yourself out of bed.

Reality #2: You May Be Considered Irrelevant

Take a look at how dictionaries define *retire* and related words:

Retire	To withdraw from or give up a career, occupation, job; retreat; discard; be unsociable; go away; go to bed; seclude oneself

Retired   Withdrawn from career; discarded; secluded
Retirement   Departure, removal, receding, fading, retreating
Retiring   Shy, reserved, receding

By the very meaning of the "R" words, if you retire you may be marked as withdrawing, retreating, giving up, departing, discarded, faded.

Small wonder that Lloyd D. , 79, a former business school dean, professor, and my mentor, wrote me when he thought (very much mistakenly) that I was retiring: "If you retire, will you continue to be attractive as a board member? I think sometimes we underestimate the importance of our active affiliation with a university. For example, as a retiree I never would have been asked to be a board member of a health organization. It was my position as dean that attracted them."

Right or wrong, we're usually defined by our careers.

Let's take a look at an exchange that's likely to occur when an "R" person meets a businessperson at a social function.

> "What kind of business are you in?"
> "Oh, I'm retired."
> Slight pause. "What did you use to do?" (Translation: "What you do now really doesn't interest me.")

Mel H., 68, a retired vice president of a large nonprofit, said that when he's at a party with a lot of "working people," he doesn't say he's retired. He feels obligated to recreate his life just to stay in the conversation. "If I tell them I'm retired, it's like hitting a brick wall. So I tell them I'm a consultant. I tell them about the projects I handled when I was working, only I use the present tense. Since I do some consulting work [he has had only one three-day job since he retired over a year ago], I'm really not lying to them."

The mere presence of "R" people makes some individuals uncomfortable. Hal K., a business owner in his mid-70s who is not contemplating retirement, has this to say: "I feel somewhat uneasy being around people who are retired. I know that someday I'll have to retire—be like they are—and I'm not looking forward to that."

Reality #3: Some Social Relationships May Vanish

Leave the workplace and you may discover shifts in your relationships with friends and relatives. You—or they—may realize the interests you once shared about the business world are no longer common ground.

Maybe, because of your career activities, you've been a role model for younger people, colleagues, relatives, or the children of friends. This admiration made it fun for both you and them. Retire and that is gone. People may love old codgers, but they seldom want to be like them.

Reality #4: You May Have Turf Conflicts with Your Spouse

When a typical husband retires, he's suddenly around the house, encroaching on his wife's territory. This can become a real source of conflict, as John H. found out. (You'll learn more about John later on.)

> *It was around 8:30 or 9:00 o'clock of the first day of my retirement. I went down the stairs to start making some phone calls. My wife said, "I hope you're not going to be using the phone. Remember, you're on my turf now." That was her time to make phone calls— she'd been doing this for years. This was the start of our turf conflicts. . . . There are a lot of things you have to do differently."*

A turf conflict over the telephone?
Sounds trivial, doesn't it?

But these little difficulties add up. It could wind up in the situation Mary N. describes:

> *My first marriage was working out okay. We had three children. I stayed home and took care of the kids; he worked. Then he retired. He was around the house all the time. He drove me nuts. When I'd go to the store, he was standing at the door. When I'd come home, there he'd be at the door. It got so I couldn't stand it. I got a divorce.*

Retirement can create problems no matter what the spouse's career. Consider the case of Carl K., 65, a former English professor at a major university. Carl's wife, Kate, was a designer and a poet who worked at home. She had no thoughts of retiring. When Carl retired, she found him tinkering around the house and gardening—and, to be sure, he was there for lunch. Kate's reaction? "You're in my face, in my space." And regardless of how Carl tried to make accommodations, he didn't always succeed.

"In my face, in my space" isn't the worst complication. If your significant other gives up a career to accommodate your plans, even more pain can result.

Al O. retired at the age of 65. He wanted to travel part of the year and spend most of the remaining time in a vacation condo. Of course, he wanted Helen, his wife, to be with him. However, Helen, 12 years younger, had a career and wanted to continue working. To accommodate Al, Helen quit her job. The outcome? Much of the time she feels "lost" and "very frustrated."

Reality #5: Your Self-Esteem May Drop

As you've seen, when you're retired you risk losing a sense of accomplishment, prestige, and social relationships. Top those off with possible turf conflicts with your significant other, and is it any wonder you find your self-esteem shrinking?

Gerontologists say a lack of self-esteem is more damaging than failing health, loneliness, or poverty!

What Can You Do?

All in all, even thinking about retirement can be pretty depressing. As one ex-CEO put it, "You get an empty feeling—a feeling of being somewhat obsolete. And this feeling doesn't get any better."

Since you're reasonably secure financially, retirement will allow you to spend more time with family and friends, pursue your hobbies, travel. Your life might be tolerably content.

But think about it: *Spending the rest of your life feeling somewhat obsolete and just tolerably content!*

Of course there are worse predicaments. But is this what you want? You may have 20, 30, or even 40 more years to live. That's quite a haul.

So what can you do?

First, purge *retire, retired, retirement,* and *retiring* from any self-description. Think of yourself as receding, fading, withdrawn from a career, and it'll become a self-fulfilling prophecy—you'll hit that brick wall. Use those "R" words only in describing others.

Second, don't think of yourself as leaving a high-energy, focused life. Rather, think of yourself as *starting* a new life—a renewal. A rebirth that will give you excitement, enlightenment, and energy. Yes, a *renaissance.*

What all this means, of course, is that it's okay for you to leave your job, but you can't *retire.*

About This Book

In the summer of 2000, I left a long career as a tenured professor of marketing. I could have hung on for many more years. Yet I quit.

I wanted to learn how people could have an invigorating, enthusiastic life if traditional retirement wasn't for them. This was my goal, and this book is the result of what I discovered.

Since I started my research, I've read about, observed, and talked with hundreds of people in the so-called retirement age bracket. I focused my study on those like you and me—neither the very rich and very famous nor those struggling to make ends meet. I write about many people with socioeconomic and demographic backgrounds similar to yours, and I think you'll find that they share a number of your concerns and values.

Some of the people had no thoughts of retiring even though they were beyond the so-called retirement age. Some were contemplating retirement. Some were already retired. Some of them found the transition to this new period of life relatively painless. Others struggled, sometimes for years, to find a meaning for their existence. Some never found a fulfilling life.

Gradually, patterns began to emerge. Although the people I studied shared certain age and economic similarities, they were vastly different in terms of previous occupation, temperament, and geographic location. Yet those who were excited about life shared common ground. Those who found this stage of life troublesome also shared common ground, but their commonalties were diametrically different from the other group's.

The patterns that unfolded were the genesis of the journey to renaissance spelled out in this book. I've arranged them in a six-step procedure:

STEP 1 *The propellant:* know the driving force of a renaissance.

STEP 2 *The clues:* learn from the successes and failures of others.

STEP 3 *The target:* zero in on the object of your search.

STEP 4 *The paths:* explore alternative ways to your renaissance.

STEP 5 *The plan:* make your renaissance a reality.

STEP 6 *The communication:* give your renaissance the standing it deserves.

Throughout this book, I use real experiences of real people. Theories are fun to develop and sometimes interesting to listen to, but as you know, they're highly suspect until they're tested. All of the ideas here have been tested in the "field"—that is, in people's own lives.

In case you need additional information, Appendix A offers references to easy-to-access sources that will help you in your search for the right path. If you are looking for ideas to stimulate your thinking about renaissance activities, Appendix B will give you scores of suggestions. Appendix C has useful forms and an explanatory case example.

Now let's get started by taking a closer look at *the propellant:* the driving force of a renaissance.

The Propellant
Know the Driving Force

When you see a purpose and meaning in what you're doing, you become more excited, enthusiastic, and energetic. At the same time, your problems of today and your fears of tomorrow become less foreboding. As the philosopher Friedrich Nietzsche wrote, "He who has the why to live can bear almost any how."

For our purposes, the point is obvious:

To energize your renaissance you need a "why."

Consider the "whys" that propel Irv T., John H., and Gib J.

Irv T.

Irv retired when he was 70. He had spent his life working for his family's scrap iron business, ultimately as CEO. He found himself losing interest in his job and decided it was time to get out, so he turned the business over to his son. But Irv didn't have a clear idea of what he wanted to do next. Soon he became depressed.

Then Irv's doctor suggested he become serious about his hobby—art. Irv now spends about four hours a day painting. He has found a new "why." Listen to Irv:

What I'm doing is something I could be remembered for. When I'm gone, people may say, "It was after he quit his job that he took up sketching."

John H.

John, 63, left his job for more upbeat reasons. The CEO of a thriving bottled water company, he retired in his early 60s so he could relax and enjoy himself. He especially looked forward to playing more golf. Within a few months, however, he felt dissatisfied.

John's dream of nonstop relaxation just didn't work out. Nor, as he observes, has it worked for many other retirees who have the same objective:

> *Usually they think that Year 1 is great, Year 2 is so-so. By Year 3 they're starting to struggle with issues such as "Who am I?" "Where am I going?" and "Why am I doing this?"*

Not surprisingly, John jumped at the news that one of his son's friends was starting a scientific equipment company and needed someone to take charge of day-to-day operations. Now John is the chief operating officer (COO) of the fledgling firm. He plays golf on weekends—and enjoys it more than when he was retired and playing every day.

Gib J.

Gib's reasons for leaving his job as superintendent of power-line construction for a southwestern state were entirely economic. In his early 60s, Gib was offered an early retirement package that was too good to turn down. But Gib already knew that the traditional retirement was not what he wanted.

Gib managed to combine the best of both worlds. He became a sales representative, selling epoxy coatings to power companies, but arranged it so he could make his calls while touring the Southwest with his wife in their luxurious RV.

These three men had different reasons for leaving their jobs: loss of enthusiasm, a need for more personal time, an early retirement package. But Irv and John ran into a brick wall: they discovered—as Gib already knew—that retirement can bring no sense of meaning, no special reason to jump-start mornings, no "why" for living.

However, Irv, John, and Gib didn't let it end there. They found careers that became the focal point of their renaissance. Their careers brought significance to their lives and gave them a reason to look forward to each day. Their careers gave them a "why" for their existence.

You, too, need a career that will bring passion to your life.

But can we really say that Irv's painting and Gib's tooling around the Southwest in his RV while making sales calls—each one working only about 20 hours per week—are "careers"?

You bet.

Dictionaries define a career as a chosen profession, calling, or mission, which you pursue through part or all of your life. The passion you bring to your work is the defining factor. Whatever your age when you take up that work, and however much time you spend on it, if you approach it as a career, it becomes a career.

Lucky You

I told a friend about the careers of Irv, the painter, and Gib, the manufacturer's representative.

My friend said to me, somewhat sarcastically, "If you're only working two to three days a week, you don't have a career. You're retired."

I asked him, "Would you call a 30-year-old person 'retired' if he could do his job in two to three days and then play golf the rest of the week?"

My friend thought for a moment. "No, I wouldn't call him 'retired,' I'd call him 'lucky.'"

Now's your time to be "lucky."

The Pie Is Yours to Slice

Take a look at the pie charts, A and B. During your previous career, your days probably were portioned out like Pie Chart A.

Pie Chart A

Most of your time was spent on your career. Your "free time"
slice was probably so small it wouldn't have made a good
late-night snack. Because of that huge chunk of time con-
sumed by career, you probably missed many of your kids'
soccer games, birthday parties, and golf trips with friends.

But take a look at your pie chart now.

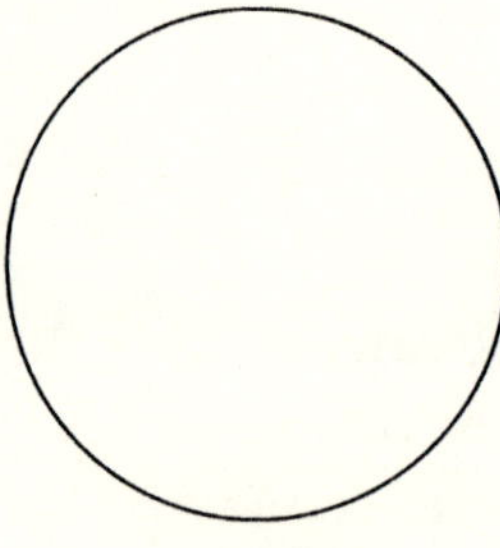

Pie Chart B

It's blank!

You can cut up the pie in any way you want. There's no
"must" or "should" anymore. You've paid your dues. You
now have more control over your life.

Your career—albeit central—is only one component of your
renaissance. You can tailor your career so that you can do

many things that formerly seemed out of the question. Since you're reasonably secure financially, you can slice off as much—or as little—time as you like for your career. It's your call.

You can spend time getting to know your family better, take that long-deserved vacation, read books to satisfy your intellectual craving, exercise, play tennis, go hiking, or even find a new place to live.

Tom W., 62, formerly a vice president of sales for a computer software company, now consults two days a week. He claims: "To me, jumping out of bed to work on a project or jumping out of bed because I have other things to do is cool. But sometimes it's just as cool to be able to stay in bed because I want to."

Rick R., 58, quit his legal profession to make high-end bamboo fly fishing rods. He works about 20 hours a week in a studio in back of his house, except during the trout season when he works very little, or during musket-loading deer hunting season when he doesn't work at all.

Your Career Is Yours to Pick

This time around, it's not your father-in-law's approval or the kids' college funds that will determine what kind of career you'll have. You can choose a career that will give you deep personal satisfaction and still allow you to live, to the fullest, other important aspects of your life.

Tony T., at the age of 70, quit his former career as art director for an advertising agency and became a freelance artist. Now 78, here's how he feels about the change:

When I left the corporate world, it was the end of one phase of my life; I then entered into another era. I'm more excited now than I was in my previous career.

Now I can do what I want to do and when I want to do it. I work three to six hours a day. I'm now working more vigorously and with more purpose because I'm working on what I want to—I'm stretching myself. . . . And now that I'm carving marble, the passion is insatiable.

Do you like remodeling homes? Have you always wanted to write? Paint? Perhaps you've been eager to give back to your community by counseling small businesses.

Or you might decide to revamp your present career, as Vernon P., 72, did. He sold his lumber yard, quit commercial real estate development, and now concentrates on what he likes—residential real estate. What does Vernon think about his new career? "When I wake up in the morning, I jump out of bed. I'm more excited about my business now than I was 20 years ago!"

Yes, you now can do what you want to do and spend your time the way you want to. Like the phoenix, you can be born again.

Too Old to Be Reborn?

No way!

Let's look at the reasons why.

The Myth of Aging

The belief that people suddenly become old at 65 is a too commonly accepted illusion. The supposed mental deterioration of the 65-plus—wilting creativeness and loss of memory—seems to be the major reason for this idea. Yet evidence reveals that it's just a myth. For example:

As far back as 1957, a group of noted scientists, including Erich Fromm, Abraham Maslow, Margaret Mead, and Carl

Rogers, participated in seminars on creativity at the University of Michigan. Age was not identified as an issue.

In 1999, *ScienceDaily* reported a study by Rotman Research Institute in conjunction with Toronto and Brandeis Universities, revealing that the resiliency of older people's brains is greater than previously believed. For example, there were no significant differences in the results of short-term memory tests between older and younger subjects. The older people simply tended to rely on different sections of the brain than those who were younger.

Kausler and Kausler, in *Graying of America* (2001), cite test results on comprehension and memory. In these tests, the scores of professors in their 60s equaled those of professors who were 30 years younger.

Dr. Jeffery M. Schwartz and Sharon Begley (2002) report research revealing that the parts of the brain that are used the most expand. Furthermore, the brain can rewire itself. These findings give new insights into the way we age.

As Leonard Hayflick noted, "Chronological age is an unreliable measure of aging—but a proven measure of the passage of time called birthdays and receiving presents."

Nonagenarian Role Models

Look around and you'll find no lack of examples.

Charles H., 91, has been practicing law since 1931. He enjoys his practice because he likes to "scrap" intellectually. Of course, the money he earns also helps make working pleasurable.

Haskell C., 93, is CEO of Stillwater Milling, a $40-million company with 150 employees. Starting as a bookkeeper during the Depression, Haskell became CEO in 1971. Very much in command, he is at his office six days a week—often sitting at a computer studying grain prices. But Haskell doesn't just dwell in the present. He's also preparing the company for the future through technology, innovation, and diversification.

Walter W., 90, is chief of obstetrics and gynecology at University Hospital in Augusta, Georgia. Although he isn't "catching babies" anymore, he still does minor operations and often makes house calls.

Philip J., a renowned architect, continues to work at 94. Some of his designs include the IDS Center in Minneapolis, Pennzoil Place in Houston, and the AT&T (now Sony) building in Manhattan. Which design interests him most? "The next one I'm doing—my whole horizon is on that building." At one time he felt that "old people had little to offer." Now he has a different opinion.

Of course, we all know of Strom Thurmond, who at 100 was still a United States senator. And this is young compared to Robert E. In 1968, when Robert was a mere 70, he sold the zipper company he co-founded in 1954. But Robert got bored in retirement. So when the company asked him to come back as a consultant, he gladly accepted.

Now, at the age of 102, with the help of a live-in assistant, he's still working two days a week: watching over employees, negotiating with vendors, overseeing long-standing accounts. His long-time experience makes him a very valuable consultant.

Chalk Up the Benefits

Let's face it. Having a career at this stage in life may challenge conventional thinking. Chances are, the very thought of working past the age when you "should" stop might make you feel out of step.

But embarking on a new career or continuing your old one actually puts you very much on the cutting edge. A 2002 study by AARP revealed that 69 percent of workers 45 and older plan to work in some manner during their "retirement" years.

In step or out of step, there are at least two compelling reasons why you should stay with your present career or start a new one:

- ➤ *Quality of life*
- ➤ *Quantity of life*

These two reasons make it unmistakably clear that there's no time for retirement.

Compelling Reason #1: Quality of Life

Albert Schweitzer claimed, "The best medicine I had is the knowledge that I had a job to do."

Recall the nonagenarians?

For Charles, his medicine is practicing law. For Haskell, it's running Stillwater Mining. For Walter, it's being chief of obstetrics and gynecology. For Philip, it's designing buildings.

Do they have feelings of obsolescence? Of course not.

Nor do they have time to brood about their mortality. Their careers keep them too busy. they have careers they *must live for.*

Having something you must live for helps overcome the negatives of retirement we talked about earlier: Having a career can give you a sense of accomplishment and relevancy, facilitate social relationships, and even reduce turf conflicts with your spouse. These all build your self-esteem. But equally important, having a career can help you sustain mental agility.

For example, as reported in the *Journal of Gerontology: Social Sciences,* researchers found that productive activity (not "busy" activity, but *productive* activity) was essential for successful aging.

A Harvard University study tested physicians over 65, both those who were still practicing medicine and those who were retired, on a number of mental tasks. The average scores were higher for those physicians who were still active in their practice than for those who were retired.

Studies of young animals by the eminent neuroscientist Dr. Marion Diamond revealed that those with stimulating environments grew new brain cells. Those in stimulus-deprived surroundings, on the other hand, suffered brain-cell deterioration. Experiments have shown similar results with middle-aged animals. These findings led Dr. Diamond to believe that the brains of older people can retain flexibility and vitality. Dr. Diamond has no thoughts of retiring.

Such studies have led one researcher, Scott Rex, to conclude that a person grows old not because of chronological age, but by lack of purpose causing idleness in the mind and body: "We decline and decay by abandoning our flexibility, our ideals, our talents, our life's mission, and our involvement in our community. We grow old and retire by buying into society's story that we can be surplused, junked, and discarded."

Compelling Reason #2: Quantity of Life

With your renaissance, not only will your quality of life improve, but you may even be around longer to enjoy it. We can't escape death. But—and this is a big *but*—how long we live is something we can, within limits, control.

A team of miners, trapped underground by the collapse of a mine shaft, were awaiting rescue. They knew that oxygen in the trapped area was limited. How much time they had before the supply would be exhausted was unknown.

Only one miner had a watch. The others asked him to let them know when each hour passed. Wanting to give them hope and not cause panic, the person with the watch gave them "hourly calls," but only after two hours had actually elapsed. The miners were eventually rescued. Only one didn't survive—the one with the watch.

John Adams and Thomas Jefferson, on their death beds for months, both had a burning desire to live until the 50th anniversary of the signing of the Declaration of Independence. On that day, John Adams, 90, and Thomas Jefferson, 83, died.

Such anecdotes are backed by scores of studies. A sampling:

A 25-year study sponsored by the National Institutes of Health found that highly organized activity was a strong predictor of longevity and vitality, second only to abstinence from smoking. Research conducted by Duke University found that in the United States, out of 788 factors, the top predictor for long life was work satisfaction.

Deepak Chopra and Sherwin B. Nuland report that seemingly healthy men who retire and are removed from intellectual stimulation and physical activity increase their risk for heart attacks and cancer. Death often follows. This demise has been dubbed "early retirement death." The root cause seems to be the belief that one's productive days are over. On the other hand, some people with enduring health problems survive into their 90s because they have goals they feel must be accomplished.

Research by insurance companies reveals that businessmen and military officers who retire to "live the good life" survive only about six to seven years past retirement.

These studies strongly suggest that, to function properly, your immune system needs a signal—a sign from your brain that you believe your life is worth the fight. This faith becomes more and more important as you grow older.

Add up the facts. Have a "why" and you'll probably age more gracefully and may even stick around longer.

Meeting the Challenges

You and I know that you're going to encounter some hurdles higher than you've been accustomed to. More aches. More pains. More losses of those you love. Will you dwell on these raised bars, or will you be possessed by that "why"?

Lack vitality? Then design a career that helps you focus on tasks that rev up your energy and enthusiasm. As Charles Schulz, the creator of *Peanuts*, put it, "Life is like a ten-speed bike. Most of us have gears we never use."

Sure, there are some things you can't do as well as you could when you were younger, but experience enables you to do others better. And you can put setbacks in better perspective.

Start Now

You may have an excuse for putting off planning your renaissance. Perhaps it's one of the excuses I've heard time and again:

- ➤ "I'm still working. When I quit my job I'll have more time."
- ➤ "I've got a lot of little things to do. Get my cell phone changed. Get my PC hooked up. Get my health plan in place. Stuff like that. After six months or so, when I get all these other things out of the way, then I'll start asking, 'Now what?'"
- ➤ "My life's been structured for so long. After I quit my job I'm going to relax for a while."
- ➤ "I'm going on a vacation in a couple of weeks. After I get back . . ."

You'll probably never receive the clear signal, *"Now's the time to plan my new life."* Nor will you ever "find time" to give serious thought to building a new career.

You've got to *make* time.

If you wait until tomorrow, chances are that when tomorrow comes, you'll find an excuse to wait until the next day. And when that day comes, it will be even easier to put the matter off. You can keep making excuses forever.

"I never lost a ball game," said Bobby Layne, former quarterback for the Detroit Lions. "I only ran out of time."

Don't run out of time. Put excuses aside. Start planning for your renaissance now.

The next step, "The Clues: Learn from the Successes and Failures of Others," is where you should begin.

The Clues

Learn from the Successes and Failures of Others

Unfortunately, there's no pat formula to lead you to your renaissance. Tom W., the consultant, put it very well: "It's almost an unknown because it's different for every person. For example, my brother doesn't work for money. I don't either. Yet what he wants from his career is different from what I want from mine."

Although objectives may vary, people who have successful renaissances tend to follow certain rules. They think and act differently from others.

Successes—and failures—leave clues.

Seven Clues

Let's look at seven clues that can help steer you toward your renaissance.

Clue #1: Let Go of the Past

Since leaving your business or job usually marks the end of an era, it's natural that you'll feel reluctant to let go of the past. Your job was probably close to being the core of your life.

Most likely your co-workers will be aware of your feelings. They'll say, "Hey, let's keep in touch." "Call and let us know how things are going with you." "Do you mind if we call you now and then for advice?" These phrases, although well intentioned, are hollow. It doesn't matter how illustrious you may have been.

Consider the story of Paul C.

Paul's ground-breaking research on the analysis of marketing functions—personal selling, advertising, logistics—and the costs of marketing helped lay the foundation for new understandings of marketing. Scholars considered him one of the founders of the modern-day field.

He had been a faculty member of the university where I was writing my Ph.D. thesis. Now retired, Paul lived close to the campus.

Since I was teaching an introductory marketing course, I wanted Paul as a guest lecturer—he'd be a real inspiration to my students. Yet I was reluctant to ask him. I was only a graduate assistant, and I figured Paul would rather spend his time doing favors for people established in the field.

Much to my surprise, he jumped at the invitation, explaining, with some sadness, that the faculty seldom asked him to guest lecture.

During Paul's lecture to my class, I found out why.

Paul spoke of problems facing marketers twenty, thirty, and yes, even forty years ago. And about people he had known during that time. He was living in the past.

The next time I met with my class, I asked what they thought of Paul. There were groans. They told me what they wanted to hear about was new ideas, new methods, new trends, preferably from someone currently in marketing. They considered Paul "over the hill."

But during Paul's lecture the students were polite. Paul, oblivious to their true feelings, enjoyed being in the classroom again. To show his appreciation, he took my wife and me out to dinner.

That night, Paul again spoke of how he wished other professors would invite him to guest lecture and how he'd like to become more involved in departmental affairs—on a volunteer basis—but no one seemed to be interested. Paul was a professor emeritus whom others no longer considered relevant.

Such stories are not uncommon—it's easy to fall into the "trying to create yesterday" trap. You may think it will be different for you. Most likely, though, you'll experience the same type of estrangement as Paul. Unless you're going to be avant-garde and continuously active in your former career as a consultant, writer, speaker, or whatever, make a clean break. Get on with your new life.

Make it clear to your work associates that you're not retiring. They'll feel more comfortable, and they won't be burdened by obligations to give you an occasional call or invite you to the office because "poor old Bob has nothing to do." Rather, their future contacts will be based on a real desire to see you.

Retirement party? Forget it. If the party is framed in the context of "good-bye to a person moving on to a new career," that's different. In fact, a good-bye party may help you (and your co-workers) make that clean break.

Clue #2: Pursue Your Passion

Tony, the sculptor, had this to say: "My wife is a real inspiration to me. She's there for me. All of my family, my children, my sisters, my brothers all support me. I feel very blessed. Now I don't mean that if I didn't get the support of my family I wouldn't pursue my passion. I probably would do it anyway."

For Tony, his "why" is sculpture. For you it could be underwater archaeology or animal preservation or bicycle repair.

The fact that other people may think your choice bizarre doesn't matter. You'll be disappointed if you settle on a career just to please someone else. Those now close to you may change. Or they may move on. The bottom line is that your career—the core of your renaissance—should be yours.

This is not to say that you should totally ignore the needs of others around you, especially those of your significant other. But how then should you deal with those needs? How can you balance them with your career?

Let's say that your significant other is named Rachel. No doubt, Rachel has plans that she considers important—very important. Two likely areas of conflict between you and Rachel will be how you allocate your time and where you live.

Rachel undoubtedly has her own expectations about how life will be after you retire. She may hope to spend more time with you. Or she may want things to go on as they have before.

One useful approach is for you and Rachel, independently, to estimate how you should spend your time. (You could each complete the Time Allocation Worksheet in Step 3, p. 42.) Then sit down and look at the discrepancies between your two estimates and see if you can make compromises.

Rachel may think that you'll be devoting too much time to your career, instead of spending time with her. Possibly, in that case, you can plan for more joint activities, even while you're pursuing your career. That's what Tom M., 62, and his wife did. A former school teacher, Tom is now a professional actor. When Tom takes classes to broaden his acting skills, his wife often enrolls in these courses as well.

Certainly you and Rachel could do more things together when you're not working. Join a good books club. Take up cycling. Go to public speaking classes.

Conflict may also arise because of where you decide to live. Rachel may have been thinking of a condo overlooking the 18th green in southern Florida. Your new career will keep you in Buffalo, New York. Again, perhaps, compromises can be made. How about a mini-vacation place at Vero Beach?

In some cases, the health of your significant other may determine where you work. Dr. Richard N., 70, a psychiatrist, now practices close to home. He foregoes temporary assignments in interesting locations, both domestically and abroad, because his wife's health problems make it hard for her to stay away for extended periods.

Also think of how your career may affect your relationship with family and friends. For example, will you get to see your grandchildren as often as you'd like? If not, can you make up for lost time by arranging very special quality time? Take the grandkids on a trip to Washington, DC. See the Rockettes in New York. Visit Disneyland or the Mall of America.

In the end, though, the career is yours. As Ralph Waldo Emerson claimed, "Nothing can bring you peace but you yourself." You are the person who has to be excited by your career. Details are a matter of logistics.

Clue #3: Disregard the So-Called Sensible

Consider Tom M., the former school teacher you met earlier. For years Tom yearned to be an actor. But it never seemed to be the practical or sensible thing to do.

> *I did some acting when I was in college. When I got out of school, I began to think about a career as an actor but didn't know how to go about it.*
>
> *I got a master of arts degree in education and somehow started teaching in a Catholic high school as the drama director. Then I got married and had children, so it wasn't a very practical thing for me to think of working as a professional actor.*

But after decades of teaching, Tom's situation changed.

> *Five years ago, after 36 years of teaching—and by then my wife and I were empty nesters—I decided to take early retirement and start off on a professional acting career.*

Since then I've had a bit part in a TV series, done some minor movie work—including a one-line part in a movie [A Beautiful Mind] directed by Ron Howard—and done some TV commercials and some print work [billboards]. Nothing major, but someday, you hope . . .

How does Tom characterize his new career?

Exciting. I'm enjoying it very much. It's been a lark for me—I feel very young—I actually like working and I know that even if nothing happens, my mortgage is paid.

Was it practical and sensible for Tom, at 60, to start a new career as a professional actor? A career where the pay (if any) is low and the work is long and hard? A career that requires him to constantly learn new skills, from horseback riding to dancing the tango, just so he'll be qualified to audition for more roles—auditioning that takes hours and usually ends in rejection?

Of course it wasn't practical and sensible. Yet, as Tom says, these are "the happiest days of my life."

Like Tom, you don't want just any career. You want a career that gives you fire within. If it doesn't seem practical or sensible to some other people—so be it. They aren't the ones who will be doing it.

I'm not suggesting you do crazy things on a momentary whim. Ignoring the "sensible" works only if you have the genuine passion we talked about in Clue #2. Think—and feel—deeply about what you love and what you merely like. This should always be the case, but it's critically important if you're changing careers.

Suppose you're thinking about switching from an occupation where you're skilled—for example, accounting—to one where you lack skills—say, marketing research. Or moving from a familiar industry, such as hospitality, to one that's unfamiliar, like food processing? Or what if you're thinking about a new career in which you lack both occupational skills and industry knowledge?

Sure, you can do it, but it's usually more difficult than staying in a known occupation and familiar industry. The learning curve may be longer—possibly much longer—than you thought.

As a greenhorn, will you be able to maintain your passion for the career, as does Tom M., the now-professional actor? Or will you throw in the towel, like E.J.?

Formerly a staff assistant at a university, E.J. decided to combine the desire to be of service with interest in books by pursuing a new career as a volunteer at a local library. This career involved starting a job where E.J. lacked both occupational skills and industry knowledge.

Without these qualifications, E.J. was given routine assignments, like filing books. After several weeks, E.J. realized that there wasn't going to be an opportunity—at least in the immediate future—for more challenging work. Not wanting to spend a year or so as an apprentice, E.J. left the library.

For E.J., the real passion wasn't there. Neither commitment to service nor interest in books rose to the level of a passion that would sustain E.J. through the tedium of an entry-level job.

Clues #2 and #3 work together, then. If you follow a genuine, burning zeal like Tom M., you don't have to worry about being practical and sensible. You will be doing what you love.

Clue #4: Think "Outside the Box"

Remember the puzzle at the top of the next page?

Most people have trouble solving this puzzle because of a self-imposed limitation. They attempt to draw the four lines within the area bounded by the nine dots.

In thinking about your new career, don't limit your search by keeping it within the "box." If there's something you really want to do, there's almost certainly a way to achieve it.

Connect the following nine dots with four straight lines.
There's only one restriction: The beginning of each line
must be connected to the end of the preceding line.

• • •

• • •

• • •

(Forget the solution? See p. 33.)

For example, suppose you've been a superintendent of power-line construction and have been given an early retirement package. Retirement is out of the question for you. You're looking for a new career. You have lots of experience and know-how in maintenance as well as construction of power lines. And, through the years, you've developed extensive industry contacts. Working as a manufacturer's representative in the same industry might be a good career. You'd have considerable freedom. You could more or less set your own hours, and even define the days that you'd work.

But it would mean pounding the road, day after day, enduring countless meals in look-alike, taste-alike restaurants and endless nights in motels, distinct but not different. You'd really like to enjoy life and spend time with your wife, exploring new places and meeting new people.

The negatives seem to outweigh the positives. In-the-box thinking would probably rule out this career.

Of course, you know there's a solution to this problem— you've read about it earlier in this book. You can vacation with your wife in a luxurious RV between calls on customers. Good out-of-the-box thinking, Gib J.

If one of the careers you're considering would be ideal except for certain conditions, expand your thinking beyond the box, as Gib did.

Tired of going to the office every day? New technology and changing methods of doing business may let you break the mold. How about flexplace? Possibly you can work from home—or even from your vacation home, as does food broker Doug W., 69 (pp. 92–94).

Limited market for your product? Why not produce and market it yourself? This option is working for Warren O., who writes, publishes, and markets trail guides (pp. 99–100).

Have a specific cause you'd like to promote but can't find a suitable agency to work through? You can start your own, as did Don C., 67, who founded a nonprofit to provide housing for the economically underprivileged in his community (pp. 115–117).

Keep in mind the fact that your situation is different now. You're not enveloped by "shoulds" or "musts." You don't need to squeeze out the last dollar of income. An idea that was "off the wall" earlier in your life may now lead to that special career.

Clue #5: Make Sure It's the Real McCoy

Make sure your career isn't a false one. Avoid the following four pitfalls.

Settling for a Hobby Rather Than a Career

Dabbling around writing some poetry or taking a watercolor class, going to the theater, traveling, gardening, playing tennis and golf—these won't give you the fulfillment you need.

Although hobbies can generate excitement, they don't provide the kick—the feeling of accomplishment—that you get from a big project like creating a winning business plan, build-

Solution to puzzle, p. 31:

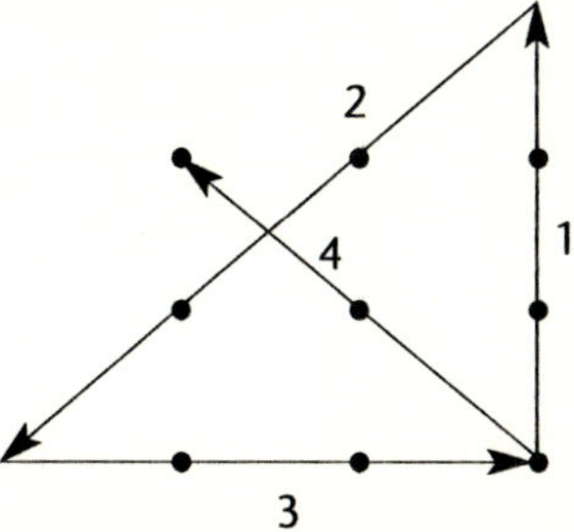

ing or revitalizing an organization, closing a major sale, publishing a novel, or selling a painting.

Nor do hobbies provide the stimulation—the lasting challenge—that you get from the "fear of failure." Let me explain that.

Think about your career, the one you have now, or the one you've already left. Think about when you prepared for a presentation for a big client, stood toe to toe with an opposing counsel, walked into an auditorium facing 1,000 people . . . the adrenaline rush . . . and how you waded right through it until you got to the other side.

No, you can't experience that kind of joy, that kind of fear, and the plethora of similar emotions by dabbling in a hobby. It's precisely for these reasons that hobbies do not and cannot provide a "why" for your existence.

By all means, integrate hobbies into your lifestyle. But don't count on their being the focus of your renaissance.

You can, of course, turn your hobby into a career, as did Tony T. While working as art director for an advertising agency, Tony puttered around with original art as a hobby. Today, though, Tony's art has a more important place in his life: "No! No! It's not a hobby. It's what I *do*. A hobby is something you do just if you're playing around, like cutting grass or whatever. Call my sculpturing a hobby and I feel offended. It's my life work. It's my expression. And it's my identity. Don't take me down by calling it a hobby."

Taking a Job Instead of Developing a Career

A job is a position within a specific organization, but unless it's a mission, a calling, your life work—a career—it's just busy work. And that's that not the propellant you're looking for.

Busy work will not give you the sense of purpose that a career does for Fred, the district manager for SCORE. Fred, as you'll recall, said, "I don't think I could ever adequately express . . . [the] satisfaction that I get from helping small businesspeople overcome their problems."

Nor will busy work give you the joy that a career does for Tony, the sculptor: "I can do what I want to do without being concerned whether people like it or not. That's me. I'm very selfish. But goddamn it, I'm happy."

Adopting a Front Rather Than a Career

The careers that some people boast about are only fronts used to impress others. At the worst, they're like the career of Mel, whom you met earlier. Mel quit his executive position over a year ago. He tells his friends that he's retired. With strangers, though, he claims to be a consultant.

Mel doesn't have business cards or stationery. Nor does he solicit business. And, as you'll remember, in the past year he's worked only one three-day job—for his former employer.

Mel has a front, not a career. He might fool others, but not his inner self. Mel lacks a "why" for his existence.

If you have a so-called career that surfaces only when you want to convince others that you aren't an "R" person, then consider it a sham. Don't expect it to lead you to a new beginning.

Making Work an On-again, Off-again Activity
Instead of a Career

Sporadic pursuit of an avocation or a hobby makes it just that. It doesn't make it your life work.

Suppose a person decides that he's going to be a consultant, but he's going to work only when he feels like it. Subsequently, he works just now and then, possibly only a few days a year. Is this a career that person *must* live for?

Commitment doesn't mean that you can't have a flextime schedule, like Abby Z., 78, a partner in a stock brokerage, who comes and goes as he pleases.

Nor does it mean that you have to work five days a week, or even every week. Joe S., 79, quit his job when he was 66. He was an accountant, and during tax season he had done part-time work for H&R Block. Since leaving his job, he has continued working for H&R Block during tax season. A consummate gardener and recreational mathematics addict, Joe devotes himself to these hobbies. But when tax season comes, it's back to H&R Block. Even though it is only a few months out of the year, it's a real McCoy career for Joe.

Clue #6: Enjoy the Trip

What do you suppose makes Vernon, the real estate developer, jump out of bed in the morning? And what motivates Irv, the scrap iron dealer turned artist, who said, "When I'm gone, people may say, 'It was after he quit his job that he took up sketching'"?

Much of their enthusiasm toward their careers is that they make them fun. Vernon strolls the streets of foreign cities looking for housing ideas. Irv enjoys looking at the masters' works in galleries both at home and abroad.

And there's Tony, the sculptor. He studies art in Italy, indulging his taste for foreign travel at the same time:

I saw an ad in a sculpturing journal telling about a month-long workshop held at Pietrasanta, Italy. It's a small town, but it's a place where the world's best marble sculptors congregate and run this workshop.

It's great. During the day we work under the instruction of masters. At night we go to this small plaza and sit around drinking wine and discuss our work and other things.

Tony goes to this workshop almost every year.

Perhaps for much of your working life you've put off "living." As Voltaire wrote, "People don't live their lives, they are always in the expectation of living."

Now's your chance. Have that fun career.

Clue #7: If You Can, Start Early

If you're still employed, it's best to decide what you're going to do before you leave.

You may set your quitting day years in advance. But if you suppose that during all this time you'll surely think of something to do—without research and careful planning—well, you may be in for a surprise. Like Pat S., a senior executive at one of the nation's largest financial companies.

When I spoke to him, his retirement date was just two months away. Here's what he had to say:

When I was 60, although my job was secure, I thought that when I'd be 64 it would be the right time for me to leave my job and do something else. I told management of my intentions, and we planned for an orderly succession.

I thought that when the four years were up I'd know what I wanted to do; four years seemed like such a long time away. But those four years just sped by. I still don't know what I'm going to do.

Months after his retirement, his wife, Margaret, said, "He never used to be home when he was working. Now he's always wandering around the house. He seems so lost."

Early planning can help. And you can't start too soon. Bobby P., 70, is now the operator of a nonprofit music school. By the time he left his former career, he had been planning and testing this career for 14 years (p. 118).

The Big Differences

Let's sum up how those who have successful renaissance careers seem to think and act differently from others. Those with successful renaissance careers are:

> ➤ *Preoccupied with the future.* They don't have time to dwell on the past and the might-have-beens. Nor do they put off thinking about the future because they figure the right plan will turn up by itself.
> ➤ *Pursuing their passions.* Disregarding the "practical and sensible," they do what they want to do.
> ➤ *Writing new rules.* They seek creative solutions that might seem foolish by others' standards—and perhaps even by their own former standards.
> ➤ *Seeking fulfillment in their life work.* They aren't trying to fill their days with busy work or hobbies. Nor do they tout pseudo-careers. Their careers are real careers.
> ➤ *Enjoying their renaissance careers.* They create work settings that make work pleasure.

Yes, successes—and failures—leave clues. Keeping these clues in mind can help lead you to your renaissance.

But what is *your* passion? What would give *you* fulfillment?

In Step 3, let's specify the criteria that are most important to you.

The Target

Zero in on the Object of Your Search

The French naturalist Jean Henri Fabre studied processionary caterpillars, so called because they tend to march in line, one following another.

He arranged a group of these caterpillars on the rim of a flowerpot. Food and water were in plain sight.

What did the caterpillars do?

They kept walking around and around the rim. Each insect had both eyes nearly closed and its head pressed to the rear extremity of the one ahead. Only complete exhaustion and near starvation succeeded in halting their futile parade.

Let *Your* Criteria Direct Your Search

Simply following along with what everyone else does most likely isn't your best course of action.

Do it your way.

Take a lesson from air-sea rescue. One of its cardinal rules is: "Know as much as possible about the object of the search so you'll recognize it when you see it."

Often the difficulty of air-sea rescue is caused by knowing, at best, only the approximate location of the life raft. To prepare for spotting the raft wherever it may be, the crew studies how it will look under various sea and sky conditions.

The same rule applies to your search for your new beginning. The more vivid your image of the new lifestyle you're seeking, the more likely you'll find it.

Of course, once you evaluate your options, you may want to revise some of your criteria. That's the nature of the process. It's like when you're entering a dark room. You have to feel your way around.

Nevertheless, as with air-sea rescue, determining your search descriptors at the outset is a real time-saver. It keeps you from wandering down many paths that—for you—lead to nowhere.

Make Explicit the Object of Your Search

Bring your target into sharp focus:

- ➤ *Time allocations:* how you want to spend your time
- ➤ *Payoffs:* what you want from your career
- ➤ *Personal traits:* qualities you want to develop or maintain in yourself
- ➤ *Environment:* where you'd like to live and conditions that would enable you to do your best work
- ➤ *Use of skills:* skills you want to use just for the satisfaction of using them

After reading about these search descriptors on the following pages, you may still feel uncertain about the criteria that are most important to you. If so, use the worksheets provided to help you visualize, organize, and prioritize your desires.

To save you time, the worksheets are short, listing only those criteria that are significant to most people. However, there are spaces where you can enter other factors that may be important to you.

On most of the worksheets, you'll have to limit your choices. This means you must focus in on what you *really* want—in fact, you should think in terms of musts, not wants. *Musts* are those criteria that are absolutely essential to you, whether because of your goals or your circumstances. *Wants* are just like-to-haves, the dill pickle rather than the hamburger.

While filling out the worksheets, use your imagination. Get in a comfortable position. Relax. Think positively. Visualize different scenarios, and try to see yourself in each of them. Work with a pencil so that, if necessary, you can modify or change your choices.

As you finish each worksheet, transfer your choices to the Renaissance Discovery Summary (p. 65). If you'd like a how-to example, there's a case history on pp. 184–189.

Even if you don't fill out any of the worksheets, do complete the Renaissance Discovery Summary. Make explicit the object of your search.

The Five Search Descriptors

Search Descriptor #1: Time Allocations

Think about a typical week. How much time would you like to spend with your family? With friends? On your hobbies? Did your doctor tell you to exercise an hour each day?

What would be the right amount of time to spend on your career? Two days a week? Three? Four? How many hours a day? Three? Four? Six?

Then there are errands and such.

Let's take an example. Humberto C., a syndicated columnist, intends to cut back on his workload. Given that he'll spend about 10 hours a day, or 70 of the 168 hours in a week, sleeping, eating, showering, shaving and so forth, that leaves approximately 100 hours. Here's how he plans to allocate this time:

New career	35 hours
Family and friends	35 hours
Self-improvement	10 hours

Hobbies and pastimes	10 hours
Exercising	5 hours
Volunteer work	5 hours

Tom W. feels differently about how his time should be allocated; for example, he budgets just two days a week for his career. "If somebody came to me and said, 'I'd like to hire you as a consultant, I want you to work 40 hours a week, and I'll make it worth your while,' I'd tell him that I wouldn't want to do it. That type of job just wouldn't allow me the luxury to have fun doing other things."

Your time is now your own, so be like Humberto and Tom. Start out by deciding how *you* want to spend it.

Completing Your Time Allocations Worksheet

1. Estimate how many hours a week you're going to spend sleeping, showering, shaving, eating (not including social affairs), and doing other essential activities. Humberto C. put the number at 70; your figure may be higher or lower.

   Subtract your figure from 168, the number of hours in a week. The difference is the amount of "free time" you'll ordinarily have to do those things which you really want to do. Record that figure in the "Total" line at the bottom of the Time Allocations Worksheet, p. 42.
2. Look over the list of major activities on the worksheet. Cross out those that are not important to you; write in others that are. For example, you'll probably want to write in your hobbies.
3. Allocate your free time to the activities that now make up your list, such as your career, your family and friends, and your hobbies.
4. Keep your list of activities manageable. I suggest limiting your time allocations to 10 activities. If your list has more, reduce the number by grouping together those with the

Time Allocations Worksheet

Time Allocations
(in hours, 10 items max.)

Career ___________

Family ___________

Religion ___________

Volunteer work ___________

Existing friends ___________

New friends ___________

Clubs, associations ___________

Investments ___________

Physical fitness ___________

Self-improvement ___________

Errands, doctor visits, etc. ___________

Avocations, hobbies *(specify):*

_______________________ ___________

_______________________ ___________

_______________________ ___________

_______________________ ___________

Other *(specify):*

_______________________ ___________

_______________________ ___________

_______________________ ___________

TOTAL ___________

(Total time allocated should probably be somewhere
between 80 and 110 hours.)

lowest time requirements and allocating one time block for the lot.

5. Add your allocated times. Make sure the total matches the amount of "free time" you calculated in Step 1. Count on doing some juggling to get your time allocations to match your amount of free time.

6. Place your time allocations on the Renaissance Discovery Summary, p. 65.

Search Descriptor #2: Payoffs

It's reported that a well-to-do American tourist, while touring Calcutta, watched Mother Teresa clean a leper's sores and commented, "I couldn't do that for a million dollars." Mother Teresa replied, "Neither could I."

What specific outcomes do you want from your career? Adventure? A sense of belonging? The conviction that you are doing good for others? Enlarging your network of friends? Perhaps you've been focused on financial goals for a long time. Are they still important to you?

Bill M., 80, knew the sort of outcome he wanted. Bill is—and has always been—an energetic and involved person. While at a United States military academy, he was the quarterback of its football team. After leaving the service, Bill went to work for a major retailing firm and over time became vice president of marketing.

When Bill was 65, he retired. But just two weeks around the house was enough. He had to be productively involved.

After some thought, Bill decided he'd like to work with young people and enjoy comradeship with others who shared the same interests. He also wanted to work close to home to avoid a lengthy commute. And he wanted to have time to engage in other activities.

As with many who seek renaissance careers, money was not Bill's concern. "Perhaps," he thought, "I can teach part-time at a

*university." He targeted one nearby. He got a position he wanted—
a part-time executive lecturer.*

That was 15 years ago. Today, Bill's still on the job.

Like Bill, have your desired career payoffs at the top of your mind.

Completing Your Payoffs Worksheet

1. Look over the list of criteria on the Payoffs Worksheet on the next page.
2. In the left column, check off those payoffs that are most important to you. Write in any others that you believe are critical to you but are not listed.
3. To make sure your choices reflect those you really hold most important, limit the number to five, if possible. If you can't do that, don't worry. Check off as many as 10. Later on, when you systematically prioritize your choices, your top five will become evident.
4. Make sure your choices have a clear, specific meaning to you. For example, if you checked the item "Monetary" because you want a career that has some economic payoff, but you haven't given any serious thought to a specific amount, do so now. Or if you checked "Intellectual stimulation," what would give you this payoff? Being around exciting people? Working on challenging projects? Doing research? Encountering unfamiliar situations?

   Jot down your descriptors in the space provided, and write in the margins if necessary.
5. Be sure you can clearly discriminate among your choices. For example, suppose you checked both "Gain respect" and "Gain prestige." Do they seem similar to you? If so, keep only one of these criteria on your list.
6. Since some of your desired payoffs are more important to you than others—even though they all may be "musts"—

Payoffs Worksheet

✓ if applicable   Descriptors

_____   Monetary   __________________________

_____   Make a contribution to society   __________________________

_____   Help others—volunteer work   __________________________

_____   Promote a cause   __________________________

_____   Intellectual stimulation   __________________________

_____   Leadership role   __________________________

_____   Stimulate creativity   __________________________

_____   Adventure/travel   __________________________

_____   Challenging, personal growth   __________________________

_____   Gain respect   __________________________

_____   Gain prestige   __________________________

_____   Use education, certain skills/
         expertise   __________________________

_____   Learn new skills/expertise   __________________________

_____   On-job comradeship   __________________________

_____   Enlarge network of friends   __________________________

_____   Sense of belonging (association,
         company, etc.)   __________________________

_____   Just doing something useful   __________________________

         Other *(specify):*

_____   __________________________   __________________________

_____   __________________________   __________________________

_____   __________________________   __________________________

prioritize your list using the Matched Comparison Ratings Worksheet on p. 47.

7. Place your five highest-rated career payoff choices, in rank order along with their scores (the number of plus signs), on the Renaissance Discovery Summary, p. 65.

Search Descriptor #3: Personal Traits

Contented people live lives that are consistent with who they'd like to be. A career unrelated to your identity will haunt you with dissatisfaction.

Throughout our lives, most of us have wanted to do the "right and best things." Yet we've faced many pressures, like career development, family concerns, and social acceptance, that caused us to compromise.

The concessions we made didn't involve choices that were "wrong" so much as choices that were less than ideal. For example, we may have started out thinking that we could improve society and make a difference in the world. In the course of earning a living and meeting the requirements of our professions, we gradually lost sight of that goal.

Often, the compromises that we made seemed insignificant at the time, or at least temporary. Nonetheless they accumulated. As a result, many of us never have achieved (or even truly sought) our ideals. Such compromises are brought to light by Albert S.

Albert was a former student of mine. He had been in a motorcycle accident when he was 16, losing motor control over most of his body. He could walk, but only with a staggering, uneven gait; he could make only guttural sounds; he could write, but the process was very time consuming and his writing was hard to read.

About two years after Albert graduated from the university, my wife and I invited him to our house for dinner. During the

Payoff Matched Comparison Ratings Worksheet

This worksheet rates each of your choices against the others. Place your choices (up to 10) from the Payoffs Worksheet in the left column below. It doesn't matter if you have fewer than 10 choices.

	Choices	*Rating*
1.	__________________________________	__________
2.	__________________________________	__________
3.	__________________________________	__________
4.	__________________________________	__________
5.	__________________________________	__________
6.	__________________________________	__________
7.	__________________________________	__________
8.	__________________________________	__________
9.	__________________________________	__________
10.	__________________________________	__________

Start with listing 2. Compare it with listing 1. If you prefer 2 over l, place a plus sign (+) in the Rating column of line 2; if you prefer l over 2, give line 1 a +.

Then rate listing 3 against listings 1 and 2. If you prefer 3 over 1, place a + sign in the Rating column for line 3. If you prefer 1 over 3, place a + sign in the Rating column for line 1. Do the same for 3 and 2.

Continue until you have compared all of your choices against one another. Then count the number of + signs for each of your choices.

Be sure to place your five highest-rated career payoff choices, in rank order along with their scores (the number of plus signs), on the Renaissance Discovery Summary, p. 65.

evening we discussed his extensive treatments and experiences with doctors. The conversation turned to the TV show *Marcus Welby*.

On that TV series, Welby, a Los Angeles medical doctor, showed a great deal of concern for his patients. During one episode, he remarked to his nurse that a patient he'd seen yesterday seemed to have something on her mind that she didn't discuss. Since tomorrow was his day off, he thought he'd fly to San Francisco to talk with her.

We asked Albert if he had ever met any doctors like Marcus Welby. His expressions and sounds left no doubt as to his answer. Albert took out his pad and pencil. I can still see what he wrote, although this incident happened almost 30 years ago:

> I think all doctors start out wanting to be like that, but somewhere they lose their way.

The writer Alexander Pope summed it up: "When we are young, we are slavishly employed in procuring something whereby we may live comfortably when we grow old; and when we are old, we perceive it is too late to live as we proposed."

Of course you can't turn back the clock. But you can start—now—being the person you want to be.

Suppose you've just met someone—and you admire this person. You want to become friends. How would you want this person to characterize you? As optimistic? Adventuresome and pioneering? Compassionate? Assertive? Enthusiastic? Think how you'd want this person to describe you to others, and you've gone a long way toward clarifying your desired core personal traits.

Completing Your Personal Traits Worksheet

1. Look over the list of criteria in the Personal Traits Worksheet on the next page.

Personal Traits Worksheet

Check 5 traits, or 10 at most.

___ Achievement oriented	___ Flexible/always learning/ open-minded
___ Adventuresome/pioneering	___ Friendly
___ Altruistic	___ Generous
___ Amiable	___ Good conversationalist
___ Appreciative	___ Good winner/good loser
___ Assertive	___ Happy
___ At peace/cherish each day	___ Healthy self-image
___ Attentive	___ Honest
___ Calm/disciplined/patient	___ In control/handle stress
___ Careful	___ Inspiring
___ Charismatic	___ Kind/gentle
___ Cheerful	___ Leader
___ Compassionate	___ Loyal
___ Competent	___ Objective
___ Conventional	___ Optimistic
___ Cooperative	___ Outgoing
___ Cordial	___ Persistent
___ Courageous	___ Reliable
___ Courteous/tactful/diplomatic	___ Resourceful
___ Decisive	___ Self-sufficient
___ Deliberate	___ Sensible
___ Dependable	___ Supportive
___ Diligent	___ Other _________________
___ Energetic/enthusiastic/ full of life	_________________________

2. Check off those personal traits that are most important to you. Write in others that you believe are critical to you but are not listed.

3. To make sure your choices reflect those you really hold most important, limit the number to five, if possible. If you can't do that, don't worry. Check off as many as 10. Later on, when you systematically prioritize your choices, your top five will become evident.

4. Make sure your choices have a clear, specific meaning to you. For example, if you checked the item "Adventuresome/pioneering," are you referring to everyday life or to certain life experiences, like mountain climbing? Suppose you selected "Generous." Does this mean being generous to relatives? To friends? Or to everyone?

5. Be sure you can clearly discriminate among your choices. For example, suppose you checked both " Cheerful " and "Optimistic." Do they seem similar to you? If so, keep only one of these criteria on your list.

6. Since some of your desired personal traits are more important to you than others—even though they all may be "musts"—prioritize your list using the Matched Comparison Ratings Worksheet on the next page.

7. Place your five highest-rated desired personal traits, in rank order along with their scores (the number of plus signs), on the Renaissance Discovery Summary, p. 65.

Search Descriptor #4: Environment

Most of us are affected, for better or for worse, by where we live and do our work.

Would you like to be located in a certain geographic location? What would the physical setting be? Outdoors? In an office? Away from home or at home? Do you want to be a power player? Do you want to function independently or as part of a

Personal Traits Matched Comparison Ratings Worksheet

This worksheet rates each of your choices against the others. Place your choices (up to 10) from the Personal Traits Worksheet in the left column below. It doesn't matter if you have fewer than 10 choices.

Choices   *Rating*

1. _______________________________________   _______________

2. _______________________________________   _______________

3. _______________________________________   _______________

4. _______________________________________   _______________

5. _______________________________________   _______________

6. _______________________________________   _______________

7. _______________________________________   _______________

8. _______________________________________   _______________

9. _______________________________________   _______________

10. _______________________________________   _______________

Start with listing 2. Compare it with listing 1. If you prefer 2 over l, place a plus sign (+) in the Rating column of line 2; if you prefer l over 2, give line 1 a +.

Then rate listing 3 against listings 1 and 2. If you prefer 3 over 1, place a + sign in the Rating column for line 3. If you prefer 1 over 3, place a + sign in the Rating column for line 1. Do the same for 3 and 2.

Continue until you have compared all of your choices against one another. Then count the number of + signs for each of your choices.

Be sure to place your five highest-rated personal trait choices, in rank order along with their scores (the number of plus signs), on the Renaissance Discovery Summary, p. 65.

team? If it's working with others, what would your co-workers be like? Make your desires as explicit as possible.

> *Abby Z., the stockbroker, knew what environment he wanted and he got it. Abby was a partner in a brokerage firm. When one of the other partners left the firm and started a new brokerage company, he asked Abby, then 75, if he would join the new venture as a partner. Abby stipulated that he would take the position "if I'm in charge of nothing, have no responsibilities, and can come in when I want to and leave when I want to."*
>
> *His conditions were accepted. Today, three years later, Abby claims, "Why should anyone retire if one has a job like mine? Besides, I like to work."*

Follow Abby's example. Think about the working conditions that would be ideal for you.

Completing Your Environment Worksheet

1. Look over the list of criteria on the Environment Worksheet, pp. 54–55.
2. In the left column, check off those working conditions that are most important to you. Write in any others that you believe are critical but are not listed.

   To help guide your thoughts, consider the positive and negative characteristics of your previous jobs. For instance, you may—like many—have detested your daily commute. If so, then you will probably check "Maximum commuting time" and write in the maximum amount of time you want to spend commuting.
3. To ensure that your choices reflect those you really hold most important, limit the number to five, if possible. If you can't do that, don't worry. Check off as many as 10. Later, when you systematically prioritize your choices, your top five will become evident.
4. Make sure your choices have a clear, specific meaning to you. For example, if you checked the item "Time of day,"

what time would that be? Morning? Afternoon? Evening? Or suppose you checked "Physical amenities of workplace." Does this mean appearance of the building? Size of office? Furnishings?

Jot down your descriptors in the space provided, and write in the margins if necessary.

5. Be sure you can clearly discriminate among your choices. For example, suppose you checked both "Variety of tasks" and "New, different types of work." Do they seem similar to you? If so, keep only one of these criteria on your list.
6. Since some of your desired environment conditions are more important to you than others—even though they all may be "musts"—prioritize your list using the Matched Comparison Ratings Worksheet, p. 56.
7. Place your five highest-rated work environment choices, in rank order along with their scores (the number of plus signs), on the Renaissance Discovery Summary, p. 65.

Search Descriptor #5: Use of Skills

Think about what you do well and what you like to do. Often people who are good at particular skills enjoy using them. Many people have found their renaissance careers by using skills they refined during previous occupations. Fred and John, former CEOs, now use their administrative skills—Fred as a district manager for SCORE, and John as a COO for a start-up company.

And when you're mulling over your abilities, don't overlook skills that you've developed outside your previous careers—transferable skills, perhaps from hobbies and avocations.

Take the case of Ray E., 73. While Ray was selling steel structure buildings, twice he volunteered as a campaign manager for a state legislature candidate (the candidate won both

Environment Worksheet

___ **Geographic Location** ___________________________________

___ **Area of Interest**

(Special area of interest such as computers, animals, plants, food, boating, aeronautics, sports, schools, manufacturing, retailing)

____

___ **Place of Work**

___ Indoors ___________________________________

___ Outdoors ___________________________________

___ Work at home ___________________________________

___ Work away from home ___________________________________

___ Maximum commuting time ___________________________________

___ Work in multiple locations ___________________________________

___ Other *(specify)* ___________________________________

___ **Size of Organization** ___________________________________

___ **Physical Amenities of Workplace** ___________________________________

____

___ **Work Schedule**

___ Hours per week

___ Time of day (work at my peak time of day or have a schedule that will enable me to play golf, etc.)

____

___ Not willing to work overtime ___________________________________

___ Flexible work schedule (time off for errands, etc.) ___________

___ Flexible work schedule (hours) ___________________________________

___ Flexible work schedule (days) ___________________________________

___ Seasonal work schedule ___________________________________

___ Extended periods of time off ___________________________________

___ Other *(specify)* ___________________________________

___ Type of Work

   ___ Physical work _______________________________________

   ___ Work with people _______________________________________

   ___ Work with ideas, concepts, etc. _______________________

   ___ New, different types of work _______________________

   ___ Variety of tasks _______________________________________

   ___ Repetitive tasks _______________________________________

   ___ Other *(specify)* _______________________________________

___ Work as an Individual or in a Group

   ___ Work as a free agent _______________________________________

   ___ Work as part of a loosely knit organization _______________

   ___ Work as part of a tightly knit organization _______________

   ___ Work with associates who have certain characteristics, for
example, educational background, socioeconomic class,
age, gender *(specify characteristics)*

   ____

   ___ Work with family _______________________________________

   ___ Play a certain role in organization (for example, manager,
owner, staff, line) _______________________________________

   ___ Other *(specify)* _______________________________________

___ Clients Served

   ___ Demographics *(specify by age, education, socioeconomic
level, etc.)* _______________________________________

   ___ Work with people one-on-one _______________________

   ___ Work with groups of people _______________________

___ Other Important Conditions *(specify)*_______________________

____

____

____

____

Environment Matched Comparison Ratings Worksheet

This worksheet rates each of your choices against the others. Place your choices (up to 10) from the Environment Worksheet in the left column below. It doesn't matter if you have fewer than 10 choices.

Choices   *Rating*

1. ______________________________________   __________

2. ______________________________________   __________

3. ______________________________________   __________

4. ______________________________________   __________

5. ______________________________________   __________

6. ______________________________________   __________

7. ______________________________________   __________

8. ______________________________________   __________

9. ______________________________________   __________

10. _____________________________________   __________

Start with listing 2. Compare it with listing 1. If you prefer 2 over I, place a plus sign (+) in the Rating column of line 2; if you prefer I over 2, give line 1 a +.

Then rate listing 3 against listings 1 and 2. If you prefer 3 over 1, place a + sign in the Rating column for line 3. If you prefer 1 over 3, place a + sign in the Rating column for line 1. Do the same for 3 and 2.

Continue until you have compared all of your choices against one another. Then count the number of + signs for each of your choices.

Be sure to place your five highest-rated environment choices, in rank order along with their scores (the number of plus signs), on the Renaissance Discovery Summary, p. 65.

times). After Ray retired, through contacts he had made in this volunteer position, he was offered the opportunity to run for clerk of the peace. He accepted the nomination and was elected. His political skills, developed from his avocation, served him well (see pp. 78–80).

Don D. is another example. Don's hobby, since childhood, was working with wood. And, as you might expect, he became quite skilled. In his mid-50s, he began planning how to turn his hobby into a profitable part-time business when he left his publishing career. At 60, Don took early retirement and started making custom furniture.

But what you do well and what you like to do are not necessarily synonymous. During the Korean War—oops! police action—I was a navigator–radar operator–bombardier on a B-36 bomber stationed at Carswell Air Force Base, Ft. Worth, Texas. Until the B-52s became operational, the B-36s were considered the United States' "Sunday Punch" in the event of a war with Russia (fortunately, we were never deployed).

Did I like my job? Not on your life!

Was I good at my job? You bet. For a while I was the youngest (and lowest-ranked) first navigator on one of the 60 combat ready B-36s.

A consideration more important than what you do well is what you *love* to do or *would love* to do. Of course, what you do well may also be what you love to do.

Myself, I love to write. Am I amazingly proficient at writing? Hardly. In putting together this book, I used over 40 reams of paper—enough to make many people, including myself, cringe about the depletion of our forests. I calculate that I wrote over 50 drafts. Still, when I'm writing, days are too short.

What are you doing when time seems suspended and all that matters is you and your work? Building things? Repairing things? Designing programs? Budgeting? Auditing? Selling/persuading? Counseling? Raising animals?

Perhaps there's a skill you'd like to develop—or learn. Have you, like Irv, yearned to be an artist all your life?

Completing Your Use of Skills Worksheet

1. Look over the list of criteria on the Use of Skills Worksheet, pp. 59–62.
2. Check those skills that you most like to use, or that you would enjoy using—skills that are most important to you. Write in any others that you believe are critical to you.
3. To make sure your choices reflect those you really hold most important, limit the number to five, if possible. If you can't do that, don't worry. Check off as many as 10. Later, when you systematically prioritize your choices, your top five will become evident.
4. Make sure your choices have a clear, specific meaning to you. Suppose you checked "Arranging functions." For how many people? Fifty? One hundred? One thousand? Would these be business events? Charity functions?

   Jot down your descriptors in the space provided, and write in the margins if necessary.
5. Be sure you can clearly discriminate among your choices. For example, suppose you checked both "Entertaining" and "Inspiring." Do they seem similar to you? If so, keep only one of these criteria on your list.
6. Since some of the skills you'd like to use are more important to you than others—even though they all may be "musts"—prioritize your list using the Matched Comparison Ratings Worksheet, p. 63.
7. Place your five highest-rated use-of-skills choices, in rank order along with their scores (the number of plus signs), on the Renaissance Discovery Summary, p. 65. Also rate your proficiency for each of these skills, using a scale of 1 to 10 (10 being the highest level of proficiency).

Use of Skills Worksheet

Working with Data: Collection and Analysis

____   Designing research methodology___________________________
____   Doing field research ___________________________________
____   Researching secondary sources __________________________
____   Compiling data _______________________________________
____   Organizing data_______________________________________
____   Recording data____
____   Analyzing data _______________________________________
____   Storing data ____
____   Retrieving data_______________________________________
____   Other *(specify)* _____________________________________

Working with Concepts: Developing Programs and Analysis

____   Conceptualizing/designing programs _______________________
____   Setting up systems_____________________________________
____   Estimating costs _____________________________________
____   Budgeting ____
____   Accounting (routine procedures) _________________________
____   Analyzing/auditing results _____________________________
____   Controlling costs ____________________________________
____   Reducing costs_______________________________________
____   Troubleshooting______________________________________
____   Other *(specify)* _____________________________________

Interacting with People

____   Leading/initiating ____________________________________
____   Managing/administering ________________________________
____   Recruiting, interviewing, etc.___________________________
____   Training/tutoring/conducting seminars or workshops _____

____
____   Team building ____
____   Developing instructional programs/visual aids____________

____
____   Purchasing/bargaining _________________________________

Use of Skills Worksheet *(continued)*

_____ Selling/persuading____
_____ Publicizing ____
_____ Advertising ____
_____ Writing proposals____
_____ Raising funds ____
_____ Collecting funds____
_____ Arranging functions____
_____ Running meetings ____
_____ Entertaining ____
_____ Inspiring ____
_____ Handling complaints____
_____ Negotiating conflicts____
_____ Representing others ____
_____ Counseling ____
_____ Mentoring____
_____ Troubleshooting/consulting______________________________________
_____ Writing reports____
_____ Making oral presentations _______________________________________
_____ Protecting ____
_____ Enforcing____
_____ Other *(specify)* ____

Working with Things

_____ Innovating____
_____ Inventing/designing/formulating __________________________________
_____ Modeling____
_____ Extracting ____
_____ Building/manufacturing/processing/preparing/constructing

____

_____ Assembling/setting up ____
_____ Painting____
_____ Scheduling ____
_____ Inspecting ____
_____ Testing____

_____ Inventorying ____

_____ Distributing/dispensing/expediting _____________________

____

_____ Installing/displaying ___________________________________

_____ Operating ____

_____ Repairing ____

_____ Protecting ____

_____ Reconditioning ____

_____ Remodeling ____

_____ Troubleshooting ____

_____ Salvaging ____

_____ Other *(specify)* _______________________________________

Working with People Who Need Health Care

_____ Nursing ____

_____ Practicing dentistry ____________________________________

_____ Practicing medicine _____________________________________

_____ Giving physical therapy _________________________________

_____ Other *(specify)* _______________________________________

Working with People Who Have Special Needs

_____ Working with physically challenged ______________________

_____ Working with mentally challenged ________________________

_____ Working with elderly ____________________________________

_____ Counseling those with mental disorders __________________

_____ Counseling those with marital problems __________________

_____ Life-relationship coaching ______________________________

_____ Financial planning ______________________________________

_____ Other *(specify)* _______________________________________

Pursuing the Arts

_____ Acting ____

_____ Composing music ____

_____ Doing crafts (woodworking, pottery, etc.) _______________

_____ Making videos/movies ____________________________________

_____ Painting ____

_____ Photography ____

Use of Skills Worksheet *(continued)*

_____ Playing musical instruments_______________________
_____ Singing _______________________________________
_____ Sculpting______________________________________
_____ Writing poetry _________________________________
_____ Writing fiction ________________________________
_____ Writing nonfiction _____________________________
_____ Other *(specify)* _______________________________

Working with Animals

Specify type _______________________________________
_____ Researching/breeding ___________________________
_____ Raising _______________________________________
_____ Training ______________________________________
_____ Boarding ______________________________________
_____ Showing ______________________________________
_____ Judging _______________________________________
_____ Inspecting ____________________________________
_____ Protecting ____________________________________
_____ Other (specify) ________________________________

Working with Plants

Specify type _______________________________________
_____ Researching/breeding ___________________________
_____ Growing ______________________________________
_____ Harvesting____________________________________
_____ Inspecting ____________________________________
_____ Other (specify) ________________________________

Use of Skills Matched Comparison Ratings Worksheet

This worksheet rates each of your choices against the others. Place your choices (up to 10) from the Use of Skills Worksheet in the left column below. It doesn't matter if you have fewer than 10 choices.

Choices   *Rating*

1. ______________________________________   ________________

2. ______________________________________   ________________

3. ______________________________________   ________________

4. ______________________________________   ________________

5. ______________________________________   ________________

6. ______________________________________   ________________

7. ______________________________________   ________________

8. ______________________________________   ________________

9. ______________________________________   ________________

10. _____________________________________   ________________

Start with listing 2. Compare it with listing 1. If you prefer 2 over l, place a plus sign (+) in the Rating column of line 2; if you prefer l over 2, give line 1 a +.

Then rate listing 3 against listings 1 and 2. If you prefer 3 over 1, place a + sign in the Rating column for line 3. If you prefer 1 over 3, place a + sign in the Rating column for line 1. Do the same for 3 and 2.

Continue until you have compared all of your choices against one another. Then count the number of + signs for each of your choices.

Be sure to place your five highest-rated use-of-skills choices, in rank order along with their scores (the number of plus signs), on the Renaissance Discovery Summary, p. 65.

Renaissance Discovery Summary

On the next page, record and summarize your results from the preceding worksheets. You may already have filled in most or all of the categories as you worked through the exercises. If not, take a few minutes now to complete this summary. As always, it may be helpful to work in pencil so that changes are easy to make if you decide to do so.

Putting Your Renaissance Discovery Summary to Work

In next step, Step 4, there are six career paths. Use the key search descriptors you have just made explicit to point to those career paths most relevant to you.

If you'd like a detailed explanation of how to get the most out of your Renaissance Discovery Summary, take a look at the case example in Appendix C, pp. 184–191.

Renaissance Discovery Summary Worksheet

Time Allocations
(in hours, 10 items max.)

Career   ______

Family   ______

Religion   ______

Volunteer work   ______

Existing friends   ______

New friends   ______

Clubs, associations   ______

Investments   ______

Physical fitness   ______

Self-improvement   ______

Errands, doctor visits, etc.   ______

Avocations, hobbies *(specify):*

________________   ______

________________   ______

________________   ______

________________   ______

Other *(specify):*

________________   ______

________________   ______

________________   ______

TOTAL   ______

(Total time allocated should probably be somewhere between 80 and 110 hours.)

Preferences
Payoffs (in rank order, with scores)

1. ________________   ______

2. ________________   ______

3. ________________   ______

4. ________________   ______

5. ________________   ______

Personal Traits (in rank order, with scores)

1. ________________   ______

2. ________________   ______

3. ________________   ______

4. ________________   ______

5. ________________   ______

Environment (in rank order, with scores)

1. ________________   ______

2. ________________   ______

3. ________________   ______

4. ________________   ______

5. ________________   ______

Use of Skills (in rank order, with scores and skill proficiencies)

1. ________________   ______ ______

2. ________________   ______ ______

3. ________________   ______ ______

4. ________________   ______ ______

5. ________________   ______ ______

The Paths

Explore Alternative Ways to Your Renaissance

The path you choose may be entirely different from the one you've been following. You may decide on a radical change like Irv, the former scrap iron dealer turned artist.

Or, perhaps, you won't need to range far from your previous career. Even a familiar path can have exciting twists and turns, like Gib's career. Remember Gib? He's the power-line superintendent turned manufacturer's rep who calls on customers while touring with his wife in their luxurious RV.

You have lots of options.

Possibly you have a career in mind, but you'd like to take a look at other alternatives. Or, you may be just beginning to search. Whatever your situation, you can gain insights by exploring one or more of the six career paths described in the following pages.

Here you'll read about people who have begun new or revamped careers—careers that give them a "why" for living. Some people you'll meet here for the first time. In other instances, you'll learn more about people you have met earlier in the book.

Most likely, one or more of these illustrative cases will spark ideas.

Read Selectively

Since not all of the career paths will apply to you, check the index on p. 68 to pick out those you'd like to investigate.

Of course, it may also be valuable to look at career paths that don't directly relate to you. From these you might pick up bits and pieces that will be of help in designing your own career.

Need More Information?

It's likely you'll need more information. Appendix A has tips on how to access and utilize easy-to-get sources of information.

Be Familiar with These Terms

Note that five common terms—*occupation, occupational skills, job* (or *post of employment*), *industry,* and *industry knowledge*—have specific meanings in this book.

- ➤ *Occupation:* The principal activity of employment, usually identified by a descriptive title such as director of human resources, trial lawyer, marketing manager, or sales representative.
- ➤ *Occupational skills:* The ability to carry out day-to-day tasks of an occupation.
- ➤ *Job* (or *post of employment):* The occupation held within a specific organization, for example, a trial lawyer at XYZ firm.
- ➤ *Industry:* This term is used here in a narrow sense. For example, "health clubs" are considered an industry. In a broader sense, health clubs would be included under the classification "health industry," but for this book's purposes it helps to be more specific.
- ➤ *Industry knowledge:* Understanding the structure and dynamics of the industry: for example, for a specific industry, knowledge of how products should be designed, what services should be offered, what prices should be charged, and the methods of promotion that should be used.

Index to Career Paths

If you'll be examining more than one career path, mark this page so that the locations of the other career paths will be easy to find.

Career Path #1: Continuing to Work for Your Present Employer

Perhaps you have the option to continue to work for your present company.

You've probably been enmeshed in your work for years, and for the most part, that's the way you've always liked it. But lately you want to be less involved. Since you're financially secure, you think, "I've had it." So you quit.

Usually this decision is irrevocable. When the time comes for you to clean out your desk, you may be sorry, like Carl, the English professor you've met before.

Although Carl could have kept teaching, he decided to retire while he was at the peak of his career. But he soon realized how much he enjoyed the camaraderie of his colleagues, interaction with students, and his status. Furthermore, he didn't have any idea what he was going to do when he retired. Resigning was a mistake; he wanted to stay on.

But it was not to be. His replacement would soon be on board. Budgetary constraints precluded an additional position. As Carl's retirement date grew near, he became a "day counter," like death-row prisoners.

If you would consider staying with your present company under the right circumstances, think twice before you turn in your resignation. Then figure out what you like and don't like about your job. (If you're uncertain, have you completed the Renaissance Discovery Summary in Step 3?) For instance, do you enjoy helping clients, but feel sick and tired of 60-hour weeks plus that traffic-snarled commute every day?

Possibly you can remove—or minimize—the unsuitable aspects of your job. Once you've figured out what would be right for you, determine how you could realize your goals while still meeting your company's needs.

Illustrative Case Examples

Let's take a look at case histories of people who, rather than throwing in the towel, continued to work for their present companies under conditions that enabled them to have *their* careers: Dr. Walter W., chief of obstetrics and gynecology; Len W., sales manager; and Hugh M., mechanical engineer.

Dr. Walter W.

Dr. Walter, now 92, is still chief of obstetrics and gynecology at the University Hospital in Augusta. The floor that houses obstetrics and gynecology was named after him. Quite an honor.

And it's an honor well-deserved. Over a period of 53 years he's delivered more than 15,000 babies. Some of these babies were the children of babies he had delivered in years past. Some have become colleagues.

Like to see him before he goes to work? Then you'd better get up early. On most mornings he's at the hospital by 6:30. But if that's too early for you, why not try during the day, Monday through Friday? He'll be there between 6:30 and 5:00 (with the exception of Thursday afternoon).

When Dr. Walter arrives at the hospital, first it's the cafeteria for breakfast. Then it's off to the Walter G. Watson's Women's Center. "Every morning I check to make sure we have plenty of nurses on duty and to find out if we had any trouble with our services over the past 24 hours."

During the rest of the day it's administrative duties and seeing patients—but not as many as he used to. Dr. Walter says that about four years ago, when he was 88, "I decided to stop delivering babies. I wanted a little time for myself. I was averaging 50 to 60 babies a month."

If he had merely reduced the number of his obstetric patients, Dr. Walter could never have carved out enough time for himself. As he put it, "You can't even take a drive out in the country and not be worried about someone being a little late." So he discontinued seeing obstetric patients altogether. Being chief of obstetrics made it easy for him to eliminate that part of his job.

However, Dr. Walter still sees his gynecology patients, and he continues to perform some minor operations. Occasionally he makes house calls, much to the surprise (and delight) of his patients.

Ninety-two and still working from 6:30 to 5:00! Where does he get this vitality?

"I try to take care of myself physically, watch my diet closely, and exercise by working in my yard and at my farm. I keep in shape this way."

On his farm he grows grain, raises livestock, and has a peach orchard. He goes to his farm almost every weekend to see that everything is in order and to do odd jobs, using tools such as chain saws and weed-whackers.

His expertise with peach trees goes way back. He learned how to prune them in high school from a teacher. Later this teacher, Strom Thurmond, became governor of South Carolina and for a time—a very long time—a United States senator.

Dr. Walter's other outside interests include local high school teams. "I'm interested in young people and sports. I coached high school football, basketball, and baseball for seven years before I studied medicine. I follow high school sports and give physicals every year."

Dr. Walter keeps working because, as he said, "It gives me something to get out of bed for every morning. As long as I feel as well as I do now, I'll keep following the same routine."

Looks like Senator Thurmond taught him more than pruning trees.

Len W.

Len was almost 65. He was vice president of sales for a textile finishing firm and had been working for the company for almost 30 years when he announced his retirement.

"I guess the major reason I wanted to quit was because of the traveling I had to do. There were many 14 hour days, and at this stage in the game the only traveling I wanted to do was vacationing a month in Spain, a month in England.

"I was asked to stay on, in a consulting role. We talked about how I could help the company. And we decided that a good fit would be to help with sales training and other things, such as market development, with the promise there wouldn't be much job-related travel involved, and I could have time off for vacations. . . . It was a simple gentleman's agreement, 'five fingers.'

"I continued to work for the company two days a week for the next six years."

During this time Len worked with the firm's salespeople, increasing their product knowledge, helping them learn more about the customers and about the competition. At first, Len would go out on calls occasionally with salespeople to familiarize them with the customers he'd been working with. Len also helped in other areas, such as developing new sales territories.

But Len's two days a week as a sales trainer were not all that he was doing. He was also working three days a week at his sister's employment agency, placing people age 55 and older.

When Len referred to his "retiring," I asked him if he called working five days a week "retirement."

Len laughed. "No, I just retired from the 'norm'—the job I was doing."

His advice for employees who'd like to be part-time consultants: "Make up a list of specific jobs you can do to help the company. Point out cost advantages, such as payroll flexibility and savings in health insurance."

Hugh M.

Hugh, 67, had worked as a mechanical engineer for a division of a Fortune 500 company for 35 years. At the age of 59 he decided to quit.

"I had pretty much finished everything I was working on, and the company was going through a period of adjustment, so I figured, well, it was an opportunity to take early retirement, so I'd leave."

His company wanted Hugh to continue working on specific projects through a subcontracting firm. "My company's practice was to set up such arrangements through a third party. This way it avoided paying benefits, arguments over favoritism, and those sorts of things."

Hugh has been working for his company—through the subcontractor—for almost nine years. He isn't sure if he has a written contract with the subcontractor. "I might have one, but if so, I haven't seen it for years."

He normally works about half time. Practically all of his work is done at the plant. Surprisingly, he isn't usually involved in crash projects. "It's more steady slow. I can usually set my own hours. It's not really stressful."

Hugh advises those who seek a similar arrangement "to be aware of what it is that you want to do with your time, so you don't wind up doing a lot of things that you don't want to do."

How does Hugh feel about his work? "All in all, I find it very stimulating."

Thoughts to Consider

If you have well thought-out plans for a new career, or if your job is just plain intolerable, then quit. Otherwise, give careful thought before you turn in your resignation.

Maybe a sabbatical—a year in a French village?—might change your perspective.

Or, perhaps you, like Dr. Walter, can fine-tune your job. Perhaps the solution might only require flextime. Or compressed work weeks. Or increased delegation.

Maybe you can restructure your relationship with the firm, as Len and Hugh did. Possibly you could work as a consultant or a subcontractor, giving your company more payroll flexibility and savings in benefits.

You might be able to spin off part of your job, like Len, who kept the sales training portion of his responsibilities but eliminated the travel.

Perhaps you could continue to work on similar projects on an as-needed basis, like Hugh, the mechanical engineer.

These are just a few of the possibilities. Depending on your firm's policies and your bargaining power, perhaps—just perhaps—you can make changes and turn your job into *that* career.

(Finished exploring career paths? Then turn to p. 120.)

Career Path #2: Starting to Work for a New Employer

Maybe you've already quit—or have decided to do so.

There are all kinds of reasons for leaving a job or selling a business; some are vague and others quite compelling. You may have wanted to quit while you were at the top of your game. You may have wanted time to enjoy life. It may have been because you never really liked your line of work—you did it only for money, and now money isn't that important.

Maybe you took the early retirement package. Or you reached the mandatory retirement age. Or you were laid off. Or flat-out fired.

Perhaps you owned a business. Running it was never easy, but your days seemed to be getting more and more demanding, complicated, and longer.

But whatever the reason for leaving your job or selling your business, you yearn to get back in the workplace and you're thinking about getting a new job, perhaps part-time.

If you're like many, you haven't looked for a job in years. To help you through this phase, first make sure you know what you want from a career. (If you're uncertain, have you completed the Renaissance Discovery Summary in Step 3?)

For now, let's take a look at some people who have found *their* careers working for a new employer.

Illustrative Case Examples

Following are case histories of Dr. Richard N., psychiatrist; Len W., career counselor; Bob B., accountant; Ray E., clerk of the peace; and Lou P., representative of the U.S. Marine Fisheries.

Dr. Richard N.

Dr. Richard (briefly mentioned in Step 2) had held a number of positions, including professor of psychiatry at a medical college and director/chairperson of psychiatry at a major hospital.

When Dr. Richard was 69, his mother died. "I was kind of depressed. I rattled around for a while deciding whether I should quit working or retire. So I said to my wife, 'If I quit, we're going to take a trip around the United States.'"

Take a trip they did, driving over 10,000 miles, visiting friends and parts of the country he'd never seen before. But when Richard got back, sitting around was not for him. He contacted "rent-a-doc" companies that act as brokers for hospitals and other medical facilities looking for part-time physicians. The results were better than he expected.

"They've been falling all over themselves to keep me busy. Psychiatry is one of the specialties that's in short supply, especially in small cities and states. They'd work me all the time if I'd let them. I can pick almost any place I'd like to go in the United States, and even locations in some overseas countries."

Dr. Richard has been working for a variety of medical institutions for over two years. It's been rewarding, not only professionally, but also in many other ways.

"For a month I worked in Fairbanks, Alaska, in a hospital's outpatient mental help center. About 20 percent of my clients were Eskimos. I got to know the community very well, and that led to many interesting experiences. For example, my nurse's husband runs in the Iditarod. He dressed me up like a Pillsbury Muffin Man, hitched up his dogs, and off we went into the wilderness for a day.

"Then I did a stint in Montana. While there I spent a long weekend exploring Yellowstone National Park.

"My wife often accompanied me on these jobs, so they were almost like paid vacations."

Dr. Richard now has time to do things that were always shunted aside because of his former career. "I jog, take the dog for a walk, read the paper—which I never had time to do when I was working full-time. We have guests some weekends. We have a home at the New Jersey shore, and during the summers we spend a lot of time there.

"We also like to go to plays and visit museums in New York City. We have a time-share suite there that makes it very convenient.

"I like to take my three months off in one-month blocks. We do some traveling. This summer we're going to take a train trip across Canada. In October we're taking a river cruise through France with my sister and her husband."

Being able to spend his time like that, why does Dr. Richard keep working?

"I'm not sure I have the right to retire. I'm still able to practice my profession. Even though my education was very expensive for me, the federal and state governments invested quite a lot. I feel I still owe them their due.

"Then, after you spend 40 years really trying to do the best you can, it's awfully hard to give up your profession."

But possibly the main reason Dr. Richard still keeps his hand in psychiatry is because of quality and quantity of life.

"Research shows that if you keep your mind active and make yourself useful, your life is better and you live longer. For example, you may even retard the course of Alzheimer's disease. There was a study of nuns. One died in the tenth or eleventh decade of her life. They did an autopsy of her brain and she had changes caused by Alzheimer's, but because she kept busy, her brain and mind kept working.

"People vary considerably. Some can find the necessary stimulation through retirement, but others, like myself, can't. I just don't know what I'd do if I didn't continue to work—nothing in life is as important to me."

Len W.

Len, whom we met just a few pages ago, had been vice president of sales for a textile finishing firm. When he was 65 he quit this position, but stayed on in a part-time capacity training salespeople. He also worked for his sister's employment agency.

When Len was 71, he decided to concentrate his efforts on job placement. About this time his sister sold the agency. Len went to work for the company that acquired the firm. There, working two days a week, he continued to specialize in placing people 55 and over.

Those who made late-morning appointments with Len found it advisable to wear their walking shoes, because he might just take them to lunch, which meant a brisk—no, *very* brisk—seven-tenths of a mile hike to his favorite restaurant. With his firm handshake and steady eye contact—and his whole body seeming to boil with interest—Len made people ask themselves, "Is this man really in his 70s?"

Even when he wasn't working, Len kept busy. "When the weather is nice, I play golf—usually about three times a week. We have this foursome. If you like it quiet, you wouldn't want to play with us. We just go out for a good time."

And he enjoyed his vacations. "Next February my wife and I are going to spend a month overseas. We'll be three weeks at the southern coast of Spain. After that, we're going to visit my son, daughter-in-law, and grandchildren—my son works in Holland."

Bob B.

Bob, now 82, left his job when he was 60. He'd been an accountant for a Fortune 500 high-tech scientific company, but that firm had been acquired and he took an early retirement package.

His career and the raising of five kids had occupied most of his life. Hobbies? Bob did play golf a few times a year and ran the weekly bingo games for his church, but that was about it. Bob said, "Raising my five kids was my hobby."

But now his work was over and the nest was empty. In the first six months of retirement, Bob kept busy doing odds and ends, like "putting things in order and fixing up the house." But then there was less and less to do and, as Bob put it, "I was going bonkers."

Bob decided he wanted to go back to work. "I wanted to do something worthwhile. I wanted to meet people, be part of a team, accomplishing something.

"Looking through the want ads, I noticed that an industrial distributor for paper products was looking for a part-time accountant. And it turned out that the company was only 10 minutes from my house."

Accounting skills were important, but industry knowledge was not necessary—fortunate for Bob since it was an unfamiliar field.

Bob got the job.

That was 20 years ago. He's still working for the firm.

For the first 15 years he worked half-days, five days a week. Then, "about five years ago, they needed a full-time person. The company cut back my time from five half-days a week to three, then to one. That suited me fine.

"Now I only send out statements, working about a day and a half to two days a month. For example, today I went in at ten and worked till five.

"Some of the work I can do at home—they don't care where I work as long as I get the job done. Tonight I brought work home so I don't have to put in a long day tomorrow. I'll just go in and finish it in the morning."

How does Bob feel about his 21-year career at the paper products distributor?

"It's been a significant part of my life. It's made a world of difference."

Ray E.

Ray E. used to sell pre-engineered steel buildings. Now his career is a bit different. Listen to him tell it:

"Last year a couple wanted to be married in our Fourth of July parade, so I hooked a trailer up behind my pickup truck. My daughter drove, and my son-in-law sat next to her playing wedding music. He had a record player hooked up to a loud-speaker. The bride, groom, and I were on the trailer.

"My son-in-law would play some wedding music, I'd perform a bit of the ceremony, and then he'd play some more music.

"When we got in sight of the judges' stand he played, 'Here Comes the Bride,' and when we were in front of the judges, we stopped and I pronounced them man and wife.

"It was a big success—we even won a certificate for the best overall float."

That was just one of the 1,800 or so marriages that Ray has performed in a little over seven years.

But all in parades? Of course not. One wedding took place on a sandy Delaware coast beach. The couple's attire—bikinis. Another ceremony was on top of the observation tower at Cape Henlopin State Park. Still another couple came riding up on horseback and Ray tied the knot on a hay wagon. Last week he performed a wedding, Hawaiian-style, in a boat in Rehoboth Bay.

But most of Ray's weddings take place in his office or at homes.

"I dress according to the situation. I have a robe. If they come wearing tuxedos or suits, then I'll put on my robe. If they come in blue jeans and shorts, then I'll take my necktie off."

A man of the cloth? Not at all. Ray became an elected clerk of the peace when he retired about nine years ago. "I wasn't going to do anything. But I soon found out I couldn't sit around doing nothing. So I got a school bus license, but then the Republican party called and wanted me to be their candidate for the clerk of the peace."

The party picked Ray because almost 20 years ago, while Ray was selling steel buildings, his sales manager decided to run for state representative and asked Ray to be his campaign manager. Ray did, and his boss won. Ever since then, Ray has served as his campaign manager.

'I talked to my wife, daughters, and sons-in-law about running for clerk of the peace. All thought I should do it—but my wife did have some stipulations. She said it was okay, but if I won the election there were two places she wouldn't allow me to have weddings: coming down in a parachute or where people were in the nude.

"So I decided to run. We have a lot of highways and back roads in this county—ours is the third largest [in area] east of the Mississippi. I put over 5,000 miles on my pickup. And I won.

"My office is located in the new county building. I usually come in on Tuesdays and Fridays. I have two clerks whose duties are to take applications and issue marriage licenses. They also schedule weddings for people who want me to marry them."

How does Ray like what he's doing?

"Well, it's a fun job. I enjoy getting out of bed knowing I'm going to be marrying somebody and hoping that their marriage lasts. I have a picture of my family hanging on the wall, and I tell them that I hope their marriage lasts as long as ours has. We're going on 54 years."

And he's making plans for next year's election.

"I'm going to do the same thing again in the Fourth of July parade. A lot of people come—last year we had about 2,000 there. I've got some campaign pins out, and I'm doing a little early campaigning. I'm hoping the other party won't put somebody up against me. But I've won twice and I'm going to try a third time. I'm not saying I'm going to win, but I'm going to try."

Lou P.

If you go fishing in the Delaware Bay and pull into a marina at Lewes, Delaware, a rather good-looking man, six feet tall with graying hair, may hail you and ask about your catch.

It's okay to answer him. That's Lou, who works two days a week for a contractor for the U.S. Marine Fisheries, helping the agency estimate recreational fishers' impact on the fish population.

Does he like his job? You bet.

He enjoys meeting people. Besides, he learns a lot about fishing—what's running, lures the fish are striking, good locations—information important to Lou since fishing is one of his major hobbies.

Lou claims, "Not everyone who fishes catches as many as I do."

Sounds like a typical fisherman, doesn't he? But you know something? In Lou's case, I believe him.

Every time Lou goes fishing, he keeps notes. For example, when he fishes off his development's pier, he records, among other observations, the date, time, tide, phase of the moon, water temperature, the weather, the bait or lures he used, the fish he caught, and where he caught them. When he gets home he enters this data in his computer. Then, before he goes fishing again, he checks this database to help him determine his strategy for that day.

Small wonder that he's so methodical: Lou used to be a manager of engineering for a consumer products company. But when the firm was planning to move to North Carolina, Lou, then 61, opted for an early retirement package.

A few years prior to that time, Lou and his wife had decided to live in Lewes when Lou quit his job. They purchased a lot close to the beach. So when Lou left his company, there they built their dream house.

Lou is reasonably secure financially. As he claims, "We paid for our house in cash. Our cars aren't that old, and we usually keep our cars for ten years or so. We're basically debt free. When you don't have any debt, you can literally live comfortably on social security."

When Lou quit his job, he didn't know what he was going to do, but he knew it wasn't going to be a "shuffleboard retirement." He got his fish-counting job almost by accident. "My wife saw an ad in the paper looking for people to interview fishermen. I thought that might be fun. I had to take a fish identification test. I knew all of the 25 fish but one. I got the job."

One of the things Lou had been looking forward to was volunteer work, something that he might do to improve the environment. As you might guess, being a fisherman, he's interested in making our waters cleaner. Now Lou volunteers time to test the shore waters off the coast of Delaware.

Lou exudes curiosity. Besides his job, volunteer work, and fishing, Lou spends about two days a week taking adult education courses. This term he's taking a beginning course in gardening, a cooking class, an art course (stained glass), a course on the U.S. Constitution, and one on Thomas Edison.

According to Lou, "I like to learn, I guess that's what it is. When I go to the library, a lot of times I don't really have a subject in mind. I just wander around the bookshelves to see what attracts me."

Perhaps some time in the future Lou may again change careers. He's thinking about taking a course that's offered by the state to become a master gardener. "I love gardening, being outdoors. And I enjoy going to school."

Any doubt that he's a renaissance man?

Thoughts to Consider

It may be that you enjoy your current career, like Dr. Norman and Len W. If there are no disqualifying reasons, such as physical disability, quite possibly you can pursue your career on a part-time or even full-time basis. Or maybe, like Bob B., the accountant, you can continue your occupation in a different industry. If so, such decisions are slam dunks.

It requires more out-of-the-box thinking to venture into new occupations. However, because of your transferable skills, you're probably qualified for more—many more—occupations than you realize.

Recall that Ray, the clerk of the peace, was perfectly able to run his own campaign because of his previous experience as a campaign manager. Performing wedding ceremonies was new to Ray. Yet adapting to his new career was easy, partly because of people skills he had mastered as a salesperson.

And remember how Lou, the representative of U.S. Marine Fisheries, had no problem qualifying for this position because of his long-time interest and experience in fishing.

Struggling to find that job? If you haven't already inventoried your skills—including transferable ones—you probably ought to. See p. 159 in Appendix A.

(Finished exploring career paths? Then turn to p. 120.)

Career Path #3: Continuing Your Business

Perhaps your business has always been a source of pride and satisfaction. The whole concept may have been your idea; you invested in it and molded it until you might say, "The business is me." And it's opened doors to so many good things for you and your family.

It's never been easy, but lately your days seem to get more and more demanding and complicated. You long for the days when you have no more worries about keeping up with changing government regulations, tax strategies, new technologies and competition, liability issues, or what have you.

There's no doubt about it—your interest is flagging. You think, "Do I want to spend the rest of my life doing this?"

Thoughts of selling out occur more and more often. You think about doing what you want to do for a change. Maybe getting more use from the vacation home you were so eager to build. Or spending time with your grandchildren before they're off to college.

Still, you and I know people who have sold their businesses and later rued the day. Before you cash in your chips, see if you can make changes in your business so that you can have the lifestyle you're seeking.

(Sure, you've given lots of thought to your likes and dislikes in running the business. But have you prioritized them so you can better see what you want changed and what you want to keep the same? If you'd like a method for prioritization, use the Matched Comparison Ratings Worksheet on p. 47.)

Illustrative Case Examples

Following are case histories of business owners who, instead of cashing in their chips, made changes and now enjoy their sought-after lifestyles: Ted F., manufacturer of epoxies and adhesives; Ken H., owner of a specialty hardware store; Larry K., entrepreneur; and Doug W., food broker.

Ted F.

Ted, now 67, started his business over 40 years ago. It had its beginning in his college days. Ted and a group of fellow chemical engineering students were always experimenting, making products like shampoos, cleaning compounds, epoxies, and adhesives.

"Some of us decided that we should start a business after we got out of college. So one night at McGulligan's Old Ale House we signed up a number of guys to buy stock.

"When it came time to put the money together, almost everybody disappeared. But some of us scraped together enough to get started. We worked out of my basement and garage, making epoxies and adhesives. All of us had full-time jobs, so we were running the company in our spare time.

"We began to sell some products, so I went on full-time. Soon another investor also became full-time and we hired a few employees.

"But then we had a fire. We weren't experienced enough to be properly insured. We were essentially bankrupt. We had to sell out.

"Being an entrepreneur and running a business was now in my blood. So I started another company. It wasn't that I wanted to make a lot of money. It wasn't a case of wanting to be rich. It was just that I wanted to do what I wanted to do when I wanted to do it."

Ted's wife, Debbie, has always been interested in the business. When Ted came home at night, "she'd always ask, 'What did he say? . . . What did you say? . . . Then what did he say?' And all I wanted to do was forget about what happened during the day.

"So one time I asked Debbie, 'Since you're so interested in what's going on, how would you like to be fully involved?' She said she would. And it's worked out great. 'My wife,' as I always say, 'is the only one in my absence who would make the same decisions I would.'"

Has the company been successful? You bet. Today there are 57 employees, and the products are marketed throughout the world. The firm even has a small manufacturing plant in China.

However, about three years ago Ted's life took a different turn. "I went through the prostate cancer stuff. That along with my now-heightened awareness that more and more of my friends and relatives were dropping off made me realize that I wasn't going to be around forever.

"I began to think, What's it all about? Not money. And this company is not the most important thing in the world. I wanted time to do other things. So I began to delegate more.

"Now I don't go to the plant on Saturdays or Sundays like I used to. I used to stay late at night, but now I usually leave about five or five-thirty. And we spend more time at our places at the [New Jersey] shore and Sanabel Island."

But, as Ted points out, delegation takes skill and patience.

"When you start out as an entrepreneur, you get used to doing things a certain way. When you delegate, things are going to be done differently. I feel that for some of the jobs I've delegated, I could have done better, but you've got to expect that. Then, if something is not done right, you've got to be able to go with it and continue to delegate and not think, 'I've got to get back into it.'

"But it's not always easy to tell if what they've done is right or wrong. It may take time before the outcome is apparent. Sometimes—especially on critical decisions—it's tough to hang in there."

Ted, like most people his age, has thought a lot about retirement. He feels that retirement closes doors. "Sometimes I may be talking with a few guys about business and another person walks up and one of us asks him, 'What do you do?' and he says, 'I'm retired.' Then there's a lull in the conversation because we're not sure how to handle it. It's almost embarrassing.

"That's one of the reasons that retirement communities are so popular. Their conversation is about 'What did you get on the third hole yesterday?' and things like that.

"I'm not a good conversationalist anyway [don't believe him], so if I retired and couldn't be anything, that might be difficult."

Sometime in the future, Ted may bring in someone to replace him as chief executive officer. What would Ted do then? As you might guess, he has no thoughts of shuffleboard retirement.

"I'd like to start a lab in one of my buildings and work on developing new products. I'd also probably call on customers that I've worked with over the years. It means something to them to have the founder of the company call on them. Besides, I could pick up ideas for new products.

"I haven't given much thought to what my official position in the company would be."

Ken H.

If you were visiting the Napa Valley vineyards one August day, you might have seen Ken and his wife, Phyllis, in a red convertible, pulling into the Sterling Vineyard. They, too, were sampling the wines of California.

Or if you were in Stonington, Maine, the following October, you might have seen two people pounding on the door of the Fisherman's Friend, trying to get in for some of the best lobster on the East Coast. If so, you might also have witnessed the disappointed looks on Ken and Phyllis's faces when they found out the restaurant had been closed the day before.

Is Maya's Restaurant one of your favorites in St. Barts? Then in January you might have been sitting close to Ken and Phyllis. They make a yearly pilgrimage to the island.

Did you visit the Castle Brolio, an Italian national shrine, the following May? If you saw a white-haired person standing on the balcony overlooking the vineyards of Tuscany, it wasn't the Barone Ricasoli. It was Ken. He and Phyllis, with another couple, had rented a suite (6,000 square feet) in the castle.

Or were you strolling the beaches of Cape May Point, New Jersey, one month later? You could have bumped into Ken. He and Phyllis were spending several weeks at their summer home on the point.

You must think, "Surely Ken's retired."

Not at all. He and Phyllis have a specialty hardware store, a business that they acquired twenty years ago. When not on vacation, Ken works about 20 hours a week, spending most of this time on the financial aspects of the business. Phyllis, an equal partner in the business, works about 30 hours a week.

She takes care of a lot of the ordering. Her pet project is development of the store's Web site.

According to Ken, they're able to break away for vacations because of delegation, employee involvement, and outsourcing.

They have, according to Ken, a very competent manager who is responsible for day-to-day operations. The process of delegation is almost always difficult, but Ken seems to have come to grips with it. "When you delegate, tasks will not be performed the way that you would do them. I'm not saying the quality of the output will be diminished, but that things will be done differently than the way you would do them.

"You have to recognize that if you're going to have more free time, then you're going to have to sacrifice a lot of control of your business. But there's a limit to how much you can delegate. There are certain things you don't want to give up; two in particular are the management of cash and the accounting system."

Ken and Phyllis strive to get their employees involved. "We constantly ask them how we can treat our customers better. How we can have our product more available to our customers. How we can better present our product. And we implement as many of their ideas as we can.

"We also involve the employees in product selection. We send them to various trade shows. They recommend products that we should purchase—sometimes they are given the authority to buy products on the spot.

"And it's worked out quite well. A lot of the product recommendations are what we call pick-up items, such as unique fan pulls, switch plates, cabinet knobs, and for our business these impulse purchases are very important. Of course, products recommended by the staff usually sell well. They don't want to see products that they advised us to buy gather dust."

Ken uses outsourcing for accounting, payroll, and the pension plan. This, as Ken said, "puts the responsibility of keeping up with many government regulations in the hands of specialists."

Several years after they first started their business, they had accounting problems. "My son told us about this person who was handling bookkeeping for the business where he worked. We got in touch with him. He was very bright and used to run a very successful business. So we decided to use him as a consultant.

"He was of great help to us. One day, after he'd looked over our financial statements, he walked in and said, 'I want to tell you something. It's not going to be easy for you to hear. You're bankrupt.'

"I said, 'What do you mean, bankrupt?'

"'Well, you can't pay off your liabilities, that's where the problem is. You're not paying attention to what's going on here.'

"He began to lay out where we had financial difficulties, and it was a real wake-up call. Calling us 'bankrupt' was an exaggeration, but in a technical sense, we were bankrupt. We didn't have enough cash to pay off our current liabilities.

"At that time we had different people doing bookkeeping for us, and it was rather slipshod. He helped us put in a computerized accounting system.

"He became a financial advisor to us. From time to time he would look over the statements and advise us, in a very broad sense, as to what were good business practices and how we should manage our cash."

What's Ken's typical workday like? "When we first started our business I worked 12 hours a day and usually worked on the weekends. But over a period of years, I've tapered off. Now I usually don't work weekends. But on workdays, I try to get up about 6:30 to 7:00. I don't always succeed in that, but I do sometimes. I make coffee and while the coffee is brewing sometime I exercise [he uses the Pilates system]. I have coffee and watch CNBC and check my computer.

"Then I walk down to the post office to get the mail, and *The Wall Street Journal* is always part of that. When I get home I read the *Journal* and maybe make some telephone calls, and by 11:00 or so I'm at the shop. Sometimes it's later, and sometimes it's earlier, but on the average by 3:00 or 4:00 I go home.

"When I get home I don't have any particular schedule. Watch CNBC. Do a little work on the computer. Do some yard work and wait for Phyllis, who usually stays at the shop longer than I do."

How do the employees feel about Ken's somewhat abbreviated work week? "I don't think they mind it because they think I'm old. If I were 40 and sashayed in there the way I do now, I think there would be resentment. But now they know that I'm at the age where I don't—or shouldn't—have as much involvement in the business, and they accept that. As a matter of fact, they encourage me to enjoy myself because they don't think I'm going to be around very long."

A look at Ken and you'll realize how wrong they are.

Larry K.

A star football player in college, Larry was offered a job as assistant coach when he graduated. A few years later he became head coach at a small college, and after another few years transferred to a well-known university in the Philadelphia area. For almost two decades he was "Coach Larry."

During this time he married and had seven children. In the mid-1950s, in order to supplement his income—Larry has always had an entrepreneurial spirit—he began raising asparagus and tomatoes in southern New Jersey.

His farming operation grew, and he realized that he'd have to choose between coaching and farming. He decided to concentrate on farming.

Well, not quite. Although he did start hydroponic farming and expanded his land-farming operation, he still found time to get involved in several other businesses—real estate, used cars, and ice cream.

Two decades later Larry, who was then 64, decided to scale down his enterprises and just manage his farms and engage in real estate ventures. This right-sizing proved to be just what he needed.

Today, if you're driving along country roads of southern New Jersey, you may happen to see Larry, who is now 90. He's out there almost every day. Look for a guy driving a 1995 white Chevy van wearing a flannel shirt (or, in the summer, a lightweight white shirt) and khaki pants. He's looking after his farm and several farmettes, now rented out to tenants. And he's still in the real estate business—he has seven lots that he's selling.

Or he might be walking. Larry walks several miles every day, carrying a brick in each hand.

Or you might see him parked along the side of the road talking to someone. He's always talking to people, trying to learn more in his never-ending search for new opportunities. Even when he's home, as one of his sons put it, "His ear is glued to the phone." Still he finds time to read the newspapers (he subscribes to four) and watch some TV.

His major complaint about TV: "Ted Koppel doesn't come on until 11:30. It's a great show. It should be on earlier so more people could watch it." (Note: He wasn't complaining that it was on too late for him!)

What does he think about retirement? "Don't retire. Keep working. Stay where you are if you like what you're doing. Keep working because if you sit there and have nothing to do it affects your whole body and you start to degenerate— and most people don't even know what's happening to them."

Does Larry think he's retired?

No, not at all.

Doug W.

If you're playing golf at Harbor Pines Golf Club and Estates, look beyond the back of the tee before you hit your drive on 13. You might see Doug in his back yard. He'd be taking a short break from work, looking wistfully at you.

Yet not too wistfully.

Doug, 69, works out of his home. He's a food broker, in business with his son. But let's have Doug tell the story.

"These are golden years—it's a good life. I play golf two to three times a week, do some traveling, some vacationing, some food brokering.

"I work the dairy side of the business, dealing with major supermarket chains. My son is more active because he handles more products and our major account.

"I spend on average about three to four days a week working; it depends on the week, the projects, the workload. I can get the job done in this time because we're not committed to highly structured arrangements with other companies, or for that matter, within our own company.

"And we're not involved in the administrative work in terms of servicing orders, pricing—all of that is done through working arrangements with the people we're in business with. So we don't have to be available eight or ten hours a day, five or six days a week. This enables us to have flexibility in our schedules.

"Many professions and businesses demand that you work every day just in order to keep up. But in our particular situation it's just a matter of cutting back on the number of people you want to represent.

"We only represent a handful, whereas when we were operating at 100 percent we represented 30 packers. To keep 30 packers happy, there aren't enough hours in the day. We just scaled back."

The restructuring of Doug's business came about more or less by happenstance. He and his son had been through an unsuccessful merger—the new company soon broke up. Then Doug and his son set up another firm, taking advantage of their previous contacts with vendors, retailers, and other brokers.

Working out of his home, according to Doug, doesn't create a problem. "Frankly, because of the way corporations are putting more of a workload on their people, your contacts don't want to see you as often as in the good old days when you used to take them to lunch and spend an hour making presentations.

"Now they say, 'E-mail it.' For all intents and purposes, they don't know where you are and they don't care where you work, so long as you provide them with the information and the deals and the backup they need to perform their jobs.

"So it works out fine.

" And it saves hours of commuting.

"Besides, when I leave my office I can go to the range and practice for an hour and still come back and enjoy wine time with my wife.

"With my laptop and fax, I can even work from our vacation home. We have a condominium on a golf course on Hutchinson Island, Florida. In the course of a year we probably spend five to six weeks there."

How much longer does Doug plan to continue his career?

"I hope forever. The fact of the matter is that I'm enjoying it and I just couldn't imagine not having anything to do everyday—as much as I love being with my wife, Connie.

"I enjoy the challenge and learning new things. This past week I spent two days in Atlanta attending a training seminar on an upgraded computer process for one of our principals. I found it to be particularly enlightening since I'm anxious to become more than a novice with the computer.

"And Connie and I are enjoying more quality time than we've ever had. She's getting a little bit more into golf. She's also a clothing consultant for the club pro shop.

"We have a new home, and we're having fun doing the things necessary to make the house comfortable. As long as my health will permit and my vendors and customers will permit, I'll continue to do this. These are truly golden years."

Some Thoughts to Consider

If you have your own business, you've always looked for improvements to make it more productive and profitable and—likely to a lesser extent—to make life easier for yourself.

But now the situation is different. Your primary motivation is to structure your business so that you can have your renaissance.

Maybe it won't take major changes. Conceivably you, like Ted, the epoxy and adhesive manufacturer, and Ken, the owner of a specialty hardware store, can fine-tune your business. This might just involve using techniques you've used in the past, such as delegation, better time management, work-saving methods, shortening hours of operation, and compressed work weeks.

Perhaps, though, your business, like Larry's and Doug's, may take more than fine-tuning. You may have to do as Larry did and shed some of your business ventures. Or serve fewer markets, as Doug has.

The solution may involve bringing in a partner. Or even changing your role, as Ted is considering. Maybe it'll require both fine-tuning and restructuring. Recall Vernon P., the real estate developer? That's what he did. Besides scaling down his business so he could focus on what he liked to do, he delegated more to keep from being smothered with detail work.

Do Ted, Ken, Larry, Doug, and Vernon make less money than they did before? Of course. Are they enjoying life more? Of course.

There are many ways you can fine-tune or restructure your business. Give such methods careful—very careful—consideration. After all, you have a lot invested in your business. Money is just part of it. Possibly emotional attachments are even more important. Once you leave your business, you may be losing more than you think—regardless of how much money you may get by cashing in.

(Finished exploring career paths? Then turn to p. 120.)

Career Path #4: Starting a New Business

If you'd like to start a business, you're not alone. A survey conducted by the AARP in 1999 showed that almost 14 percent of baby boomers envision starting a business after "retirement."

Small wonder. Who wouldn't like to be his own boss?

Imagine putting your ideas into action without the hassles of bureaucracy and political maneuvering! You would decide what needs to be done, when, and by whom.

Your experiences may have made you an expert in one field, and maybe others. Would you like to put this expertise to work? Perhaps you have a hobby that could be turned into a business. Running a dive shop. Outfitting whitewater rafters. Having a bed and breakfast in *that* location. Owning an auction house. Selling antiques. Starting a dance band.

Maybe you've spotted a niche in the market that demands to be filled. Providing household services. Or limousine service. Or raising ostriches.

You may have once owned a business, and for one reason or another you sold it. Now you have a yearning to get back into action.

Then, too, even if you don't need the money, making some is always a kick.

Whatever the reason, you're giving some thought to starting a new business. Make sure that you first know, specifically, what you want from your new business. Will it provide you with the lifestyle you're looking for? (If you're uncertain, have you carefully completed the Renaissance Discovery Summary in Step 3?).

Illustrative Case Examples

Following are case histories of people who started new businesses: Len W., consultant; Tom W., consultant; Warren O., writer, publisher, and marketer of trail guides; Dr. Oliver G., owner and operator of a health club; and Rick R., maker of high-end fly rods.

Len W.

You've met Len on several occasions. He's the sales manager who became a part-time sales trainer and also an employment specialist, placing persons 55 or over. When Len was 71, he left his job as a part-time sales trainer and concentrated on job placement.

Now 79, Len has left that job to serve as a consultant to several companies, locating and screening employees. According to Len, "I wanted to be able to work when I wanted to and work on jobs that I wanted to."

After so many refinements of his career, what's he got in mind?

"Well, my plans now are to be somewhat active doing some recruiting—actually for some firms that I had been working with while I was with the agency."

Len *somewhat active?* Knowing Len, I'll bet he's working at least two days a week. Maybe four or five.

Tom W.

Tom is 62. For more than 30 years he worked in sales in the computer industry—first hardware, then peripherals, and then big-ticket software sales. As Tom put it, "My expertise is in complex, big-ticket sales—not commodity selling, but solution selling. Solution selling is a process that could take six months to a year. The process involves certain qualifying benchmarks, such as determining if there is a need, finding out if they have the budget, getting access to power, and so forth."

Eight months ago, his firm was on the verge of bankruptcy. Tom, then vice president of sales, was given a termination package.

"I didn't look for another job because I wanted to sort out what I wanted to do in life and all that good stuff. Besides, I was building a vacation home and I had elective shoulder surgery scheduled. In time, though, I found my life very boring. I was always looking at my watch with only the cocktail hour as my goal.

"I concluded that I didn't want to stop working. The converse to that was that I really didn't want a five-day-a-week job, nor did I want to put myself in a stressful situation. For 30 years I was in a high-tech industry. I worked all the time— sometimes I was on the phone at midnight. That made me a lot of money but also made me a nervous wreck.

"I'm not rich but financially comfortable. So I thought, if I don't work another day in my life, I'll survive. I want to work doing something, but I also want to have fun in the process."

Tom thought that teaching computer science would be interesting, so he applied at several local community colleges. "I got a lot of push-back because I didn't have a masters degree. So then I thought about teaching solution-selling to business organizations. I went to a certification class. But when I completed the course, the school never found me a job. I was told that business was bad and there weren't opportunities at this time. So there I was with nothing to do."

But then Tom landed a contract with an association to design a selling process for their sales representatives. And, important to Tom, he could set his own hours.

"You see, you can apply solutions-selling to many kinds of businesses other than high-tech. For this consulting job I'm giving them a process—a methodology—that they should be using. They've got a bunch of young salespeople who don't understand solution-selling. I'm giving them a roadmap they can use.

"They asked me to keep our relationship very informal, but I decided to put the terms of our verbal agreement in writing, because in a business relationship that's the way it should be done. I sent them an e-mail saying that this is what I'd deliver, my billing rate, my traveling costs, and that I'd keep a copy on file.

After I worked a month or two they said, "Why don't you give us a bill?' I created a bill from the e-mail and sent it to them.

"And I'm doing a good job. I put the procedures down in writing, and even I was surprised by how well it flowed. My recommendations were presented to the COO, and he was very satisfied. And then he said, 'Now we'll go to phase 2.'

"There's a sense of self-satisfaction I get from dealing with the people I'm working with. Sure, there's the financial reward, but it's beyond that, it just makes me feel good about myself. They recognize my experience in sales and my professionalism. And, you know, we all have our self-doubts. So it's refreshing to hear positive feedback.

"Besides, I'm working only two days a week so I can still do all the other things I want to do. Now that warm weather is here, I play golf. And I'm cooking now—I never cooked before in my life."

Tom got this consulting job through networking. "I keep in touch by e-mail with people in the companies I've worked for. I don't bug them. I just say, 'Hi, how are you doing?' And I tell them what I'm doing. Lo and behold, a friend of mine got in touch with me and said, 'I've got a great consulting engagement for you.'

"I stay friendly with the founder of my previous company. Just in the past two weeks I sent him an e-mail. He e-mailed me right back: 'I'm glad you sent me that e-mail. I've landed a consulting engagement, and I'm going to need some people. Could you work two days a week for me?' I replied, 'Sure, so long as the dollars are right.'

"Right now my life is in balance. I'm on a roll. And I feel good about having a career. I don't want to be retired. Those hours I spend working, I enjoy the hell out of them. I really do.

"One of my goals is to make sure that I'm working two days a week. There may come a day when I don't, or my clients may not like what I do. If that happens, then I'll do something else."

Warren O.

Warren retired from the United States Government after 20 years. Since he was an avid runner, he decided to open a specialty footwear retailing shop in Maryland.

That worked out pretty well, but in a few years Warren wanted to move out west. He and his wife looked at a number of places. They decided on Aspen, Colorado, an area that offered everything they liked—hiking and backpacking in summer, skiing in winter, and a variety of cultural events.

To keep himself busy and to earn extra money, Warren went to work for a mountaineering-supply retail shop in Aspen. There, he noticed that customers frequently asked for a local hiking trail guide, but there wasn't a good one on the market. Since Warren by now was familiar with many of the trails, he decided to write a trail guide, even though he had never written professionally.

With backpacks, Warren and his wife scoured the trails, recording their observations on a tape recorder, taking photos, and making notations on detailed maps. Warren found that putting together the trail guide was fun—even more exciting than hiking itself.

Since the guide was for a very limited market, Warren realized he'd have to self-publish it, and in addition, do the marketing. He did the layout work himself, got a graphic artist to design the cover, and then had the book printed. He marketed the book by calling on local retail shops.

While making his sales calls, Warren learned of other types of guide books that were in demand. This encouraged Warren to write other guides, including ones on local cross-country and downhill trails. For subjects that he knew little about, or had no interest in, such as four-wheeling in southern Colorado, he found others to do the research and writing.

As Warren's publishing operation became better known, several authors asked him to publish their works. Since his start less than eight years ago, Warren has published 20 books —seven in the past two years.

Warren still calls on local retail stores, though now he also works with regional and national distributors. In addition, his books are available through several online bookstores. Warren continues to do the warehousing, shipping, and all his accounting.

Unless he's working on a new book, he spends about 10 to 12 hours a week on administration and marketing. The rest of the time he spends running, hiking—doing the outdoor things he enjoys so much.

How does Warren, now 62, feel about his life?

"Great! I enjoy it much more now than I did when I was working for the government. I have more spare time, and I have more control over my life. Besides, what I'm doing [writing and publishing guides] ties in with what I like to do [hiking]."

Dr. Oliver G.

Oliver was a practicing neurosurgeon for 25 years. During that time he performed about 15,000 operations. Although he had a very successful practice, he decided that he wanted to do something else.

He thought of living the "good life"—he was an avid sailboat racer. But he wanted other challenges. He decided to enroll in a local university and get an MBA. Why an MBA?

"To be honest with you, I wasn't sure what I was going to do with it. I kiddingly said that I was going to go to Silicon Valley and hang out in bars and become a millionaire."

Actually, Oliver had harbored an idea for years. He believed that physicians, nurses, and physical therapists do an excellent job at healing people, but he thought to himself, "Why not put more effort into keeping people healthy?"

A few years before Oliver quit neurosurgery, his two sons bought a small health club and gym. Oliver worked out there with his sons. Then, shortly after Oliver completed his MBA, his sons suggested that the three of them bring together the best of their respective fields of expertise.

Now they are opening a medically based health club—a 160,000-square-foot facility with aerobic workout rooms, an all-purpose fitness and weight room, a four-lane pool, six indoor tennis courts, two racquetball courts, two basketball courts, and a physical therapy pool.

They plan to lease out about 40,000 square feet to private family practices, podiatrists, and experts in alternative medicine, as well as to nutritional cafes and other shops related to overall health.

Oliver emphasizes that he's not giving up medicine. He's going to serve as the medical director of the new facility, blending his medical know-how with his concern for fitness. What does Oliver himself have to say about all this?

"Well, I love it. I like the opportunity to work at preventive health. . . . At times the scope of our operation is rather frightening, yes, a little frightening because it's so different from being a neurosurgeon. Being a part-time developer, part-time health care professional, running a family business—the path isn't as clear as taking out a tumor from someone's brain or spinal cord.

"But it's challenging my creativity and even my faith. You have to have a plan, faith in the plan, and faith in the Almighty to help you get to where you want to go.

"It's work, but it's strangely rewarding because I'm so focused and energetic about it. And we really haven't got to the fun part when we can see how we're helping people and benefiting their lives.

"I told a minister friend of mine that my dream and passion is to have the Crystal Cathedral of Health. He said, 'Good analogy. What Robert Schuller did was to get people who never went to church to go to church. What you're trying to do is to get people who have never focused on health to come to a health club.'"

Rick R.

Like to buy a high-end bamboo fly-fishing rod that will set you back somewhere between $1,600 and $2,000? Then why not go directly to the maker?

About eight miles from Lexington, Virginia, get off the highway and take a rural, gravel road for about a mile. Take a right and go up a lane that's sort of graveled. When you get to his house, maybe no one will answer. If it's trout or muzzle-loading deer hunting season, you're probably out of luck. Otherwise, walk up the hill—55 steps—to his shop.

If he's there, and you decide to place an order, expect to wait a year or so for your rod.

But let's go back in time. Rick was a lawyer for the U.S. Department of the Interior for 28 years. But long before he even thought of being an attorney, he had been, so to speak, hooked on fly fishing—in fact, he had started tying flies when he was in the seventh grade.

In his last year of law school, he fell in love with bamboo fly rods. To buy one, he made his first-ever credit purchase.

About a year after he joined the Department of the Interior, he met Tom Maxwell. Tom was co-founder of Thomas and Thomas Rod Company, a firm that made world-class bamboo fly rods.

That meeting set off a spark in Rick. Within a year, Rick's consummate hobby was making bamboo fly rods. Rick claims it was the mentoring and friendship of Tom that "got me where I am today in rod building."

When Rick was 54, he left the Department of the Interior, four years earlier than he had planned. Two events propelled him to make this change.

He and Tom had been planning to write a book "to point out details that distinguished the really great rods from the also-rans." But Tom unexpectedly died. Tom was only 62. That was quite a shock to Rick. And at that time Rick's marriage was also coming apart.

"Those two events got me thinking. Although I was at the high point in my career, well-respected and heading up a small unit of lawyers, I thought, 'Why should I wait to quit? I'm out of here. I'm going to start, in a serious way, doing something I really want to do—build fly rods.'"

Rick started looking for a place with access to fishing and hunting and an affordable price. After many months of searching, he found 25 isolated, wooded, mountainous acres with a house—exactly what he wanted. Since then, Rick has built a workshop and purchased 10 adjoining acres.

It takes Rick only a few minutes to drive to Lexington. The town has two universities (Washington and Lee and Virginia Military Institute), and though the city is small, it's vibrant and alive, both in arts and in academia.

He's ecstatic about his new environs. "I'm doing productive and interesting work, I have peaceful surroundings, and yet I'm close to remarkable people."

On most days he gets to the shop by 7:00 or 8:00 and stops work at lunchtime. Occasionally he'll come back in the afternoon to do varnish coloring or rescaling. Some days, Rick may get up, have breakfast (if it's winter, throw a log on the fire), and just read a good book.

During the prime part of the trout season, he puts in very few hours. Still, even though it may be a pretty day and the trout streams are beckoning, he'll go up to his shop. "Because," as Rick put it, "building rods is a joy."

To Rick, putting bamboo fly rods in people's hands is almost a crusade. He believes there is no better fishing tool, and he wants to share with others the thrill of bamboo fly fishing.

Over the years Rick has developed quite a reputation. He doesn't advertise, and most of his sales derive from word of mouth or from repeat customers.

It takes Rick about 100 hours to build one rod. Typically, he'll turn out 12 or so a year. Figure in the cost of expensive materials, and well, you don't need a calculator to see that Rick could do as well flipping burgers.

Of course, Rick's not in this business for the money—although, as Rick says, "It's income that allows me to take a few extra fishing and hunting trips a year."

What does Rick think of his renaissance? "My life couldn't be better, and I don't know how I would improve it!"

Some Thoughts to Consider

Want to go into business? You've got lots of alternatives to choose from.

Perhaps you already have a promising customer base and can continue your occupation on your own, as did Len, the employment specialist.

Or you might have transferable skills that will make you a sought-after consultant in a number of industries. That was Tom W.'s case. His method of system-selling could be applied to associations as well as to computer software.

Possibly you've spotted *that* niche in the market, as did Warren O., the author, publisher, and marketer of trail guides.

You may have a hobby that you'd like to convert into a business. Take a page from Rick, the maker of bamboo fly rods. You may not have the reputation that Rick did when he started his business, but what the heck, you'll be doing what you like to do.

The best part of all: you'll be your own boss. You can structure your business so that, like Rick, if you don't feel like working, you'll throw a log on the fire and read a book.

Lack ideas for a business to pursue? Then check out Appendix B, where you'll find a listing of more than 50 possibilities and references to hundreds more.

Like Len, Tom, Warren, and Rick, you can start a business where the entry cost is low and the downside is minimal. Or you may wish to have a grander business, such as Dr. Oliver's Crystal Cathedral of Health.

Regardless of the approach you take, a new business requires careful planning, focus, hard work, and commitment. Most new businesses, as you know, disappear in the first three years. Make sure you have the passion.

(Finished exploring career paths? Then turn to p. 120.)

Career Path #5: Pursuing an Artistic Career (Self-Employed)

Maybe no one knows about your lifelong dream. While you focused on the practicalities, responsibilities, and yes, even some of the luxuries of life, the dream persisted.

Is it too late to set up an easel, grab a palate and brush, and get to work?

You've roughed out *that* novel on nights when you couldn't sleep. Is it too late to flesh it out and get it down on paper?

Is it too late to play in a dance band? Start a professional acting career? Write a cookbook?

Most likely, you have time.

Let me tell you about some others who have embarked on artistic careers and found their renaissance.

Illustrative Case Examples

Following are case examples of Irv T., painter, and Jack A, writer.

Irv T.

While walking through the theater district of New York City, you may see Irv and his wife, Jobie, holding up folded umbrellas, leading the way for 50 or so Midwesterners on a weekend Broadway-play junket. Tour guides? Yes, in a way. From time to time they organize theater tours, and the profits go to a local university.

But to understand Irv's real focus, let's go back a few years. You've heard parts of Irv's story earlier. After Irv graduated from college, he joined his family business, a scrap iron firm. Sometime later he became CEO. However, by the late 1990s, Irv had lost interest in his work, and when he was 70, Irv turned the business over to his son. Soon Irv became depressed.

"When you're in a funk, you're struggling to regain your balance. You've got to find something to do that's meaningful."

He found his "why" in painting. Irv has always had an interest in art. He started college as an art major. For a number of reasons, he decided to switch over to the college of commerce, but his interest in art continued.

"It's always been in the back of my mind. My wife was an art major, and over the years we've been to galleries and museums all over the world. And now and then I would do some sketches, but I was just doodling around."

It was during Irv's state of depression that, at the suggestion of his doctor, he started to become serious about art. When his daughter was married at Fire Island, New York, Irv took along his sketch book. And sketch he did—people on the island, in New York City hotel lobbies, at Yankee Stadium, in museums.

When Irv got home, he enrolled in a watercolor class and, as he put it, "just started doing my own thing." Irv now spends from three to five hours a day painting, or else he's taking an art course or visiting art galleries at home or abroad.

Irv has entered his work in a number of local shows. He's had successes. He's won some prizes. He sells sketches and paintings at these shows, complementing his own word-of-mouth advertising.

Now 73, Irv feels that his new career is very rewarding. "I can't wait to get up in the morning and grab my art pad and figure out where I'm going to do some sketching.

"I'm sort of a curious guy, and it's exciting to see how creative I can be. It's been an enlightenment to me that I have the ability to paint and that I can stick to it. I've been motivated because I like to do it and I have the time and the results are good. People get a kick out of my work.

"All of this is continuing to happen. What I'm doing is something I could be remembered for. When I'm gone, people may say, 'It was after he quit his job that he took up sketching.'"

Jack A.

For most of his "first career," Jack was an account executive. However, at 59 he decided that he had had enough of the advertising business. He quit his job, but he didn't intend to enter into a do-nothing retirement.

Soon after, a former business associate presented Jack with a proposal: to get involved in a gold-mining venture. Although this business was new to Jack, he couldn't refuse the opportunity to get back into the game.

However, the gold-mining operation failed, and Jack incurred a major financial loss. Nevertheless, Jack had found working on this venture stimulating and fun.

What next? After a bout of the retirement blues, Jack decided to start a new career as a fiction author. In college he had written a sports column, and during his years in advertising he had contemplated a career as an author. Now he wanted to give writing a try.

The required discipline wasn't easy for Jack. Lacking accustomed daily deadlines, he found ways to shorten his writing day. He slept late. He looked forward to picking his wife up after work and then going out to dinner.

Before long, however, his motivation increased. He took brisk morning walks to energize himself, and he enrolled in a writing class, where he met other struggling writers with whom he developed mutually supportive relationships.

Jack's first book was about the advertising business. Unfortunately, it proved not marketable. One day, though, a friend came up with another idea—why not write about San Francisco's society parties? Jack had always led a very active social life and, on the mornings after, had regaled his colleagues with accounts of the carryings-on.

Jack took his friend's advice and used the society parties as a setting for a murder mystery.

A New York firm published his book, *The Society Ball Murders*, which earned a number of very favorable reviews. Today Jack is continuing his career as an author.

Some Thoughts to Consider

Irv and Jack found their renaissance through artistic careers. Both had had successful business careers but nevertheless were willing to start new careers as amateurs. They took courses, picking up ideas to improve their craft. Through these courses they developed supportive relationships with other beginners.

Of course, many of Irv's paintings did not win prizes; in fact, many never sold. Jack's first novel was a dud. Also remember Tom M., the high school drama teacher turned professional actor, who spends hours auditioning for one-line parts. Tom's payoffs are usually, "Thanks for coming. We wish you good luck."

Failures were relatively new to Irv, Jack, and Tom. Still, that did not deter them from pursuing their passions. They all had lifelong interests in their artistic pursuits, even though they did not start their new careers until later in life.

You may have the time to pursue an artistic career, but do you have the passion? Will you feel comfortable being ranked with amateurs? Sitting in classes learning fundamentals? Spending hours auditioning for one-line parts?

If you can accept these growing pains . . . if you have the passion . . . then go for it.

(Finished exploring career paths? Then turn to p. 120.)

Career Path #6: Volunteering Your Services

Your mail bulges with appeals for help: hollow-eyed children, the homeless, disappearing wildlife, threats to the environment. Sure, a few of these solicitations are scams, but all in all, you know the needs are real and great.

You've donated money to many of these causes. But during your working life, you've been too busy to give as much time as you would have liked.

Now you have time.

Many executives, managers, professionals, and business owners feel they have been more fortunate than most, and they yearn to repay society.

Perhaps you feel that way. Or you'd just like to make this world a better place.

If you're like many, this is the first time you've ever thought of making a career of volunteering your services. Some have taken this path and in the process have found their renaissance. Perhaps this is the path you, too, should choose.

Illustrative Case Examples

Following are case histories of people who have made a career of doing volunteer work: Harold A, mentor of children from low-income areas; Dr. Norm G., volunteer forensics expert; Mark B., in charge of the building committee for a local branch of Habitat for Humanity; Al F., mayor; Don C., executive for nonprofits that improve housing; Dr. Bill S., founder of a free medical care clinic; Bobby P. operator of a nonprofit music school; and Herb H., teacher of computer skills.

Harold A.

The traditional retirement route, as Harold quickly found out, was not for him. He was in his late 50s and wanted to do something he considered productive. He decided to coach inmates so that they'd be prepared to find and hold jobs once they were released from prison.

Although the job was satisfying in many ways, Harold realized that his efforts often missed the mark. For example, one of his "students" flunked a drug test just before he was to be released. Harold says, "I realized that he didn't want to get out of prison. . . . Here's a guy who had no family—prison inmates were the closest thing to a family to him."

Such experiences led Harold to believe that he could be more productive working with at-risk children, coaching them so they'd be less likely to wind up in prison. When Harold found out about the Experience Corps, he decided to volunteer as a mentor at an elementary school in one of the economically underprivileged areas of a major city.

Harold now spends 15 hours a week or more mentoring six children. He works with them individually, helping to overpower the negative influences—broken homes, drug trafficking, robberies, prostitution—so often found in their communities.

And Harold, too, is a beneficiary of the program. He claims that he receives as much from his mentorships as do the children. He enjoys his relationships with other Experience Corps workers, but most of all, he values the gratitude he gets from those he mentors.

"When you arrive, they run to you. It just blows you away."

Dr. Norm G.

Dr. Norm had a successful dental practice and was making good money. However, it was no longer fun for Norm. At age 62, he wanted more out of life.

Fast-forward nine years. During this time you may have seen Norm. Maybe he was dishing out scrambled eggs at a Boy Scout camp. Besides serving on the county Boy Scout advisory and executive boards, he works on various Scout committees. As a member of the property committee, for instance, he helps ensure that the camp grounds are in good repair, and on overnight weekends he often helps cook.

Perhaps, on a visit to Israel, you happened to tour a military base, and you noticed a distinguished-looking person replacing tank treads. It may have been Norm. He's served six three-week tours as a volunteer in the Israeli army. He says: "All I do is menial work, but it's so interesting, meeting all different kinds of people. And I get time to visit various parts of Israel."

If you have stopped in on Thursdays at a regional recycling center, you may have seen Norm separating plastic containers from the rest of the recycled materials—a filthy job. Or perhaps you've read about Norm lecturing to schools on drug abuse. Or you may have seen him working the local polls for his political party.

If you went to a session of the township's deer-control committee, you may have heard Norm, the chairman, explaining to citizens why birth control isn't practical for reducing the deer population. You may also have noticed him hanging out at the township's volunteer fire company, or watched him pitch softball in his spare time (he's the captain and coach of a softball team whose average age is 28).

In the state capital, you may have bumped into Norm during the one day a month he serves as an orthodontics consultant to the state department of public welfare. If you asked him why he bothered with this consulting, Norm probably told you, "I don't want to lose touch with dentistry."

But all of these activities are just Norm's hobbies or avocations. Ask Norm what he really does and you'll get a quick answer: "Chief Deputy Coroner."

While Norm was practicing dentistry, he also taught at a prestigious university. There he met another professor who got him interested in dental forensics. Listen to Norm's enthusiastic discussion of this career:

"I joined the state dental identification society as a hobby. We did a case now and then and had some drills. At the time I had no idea that this would lead me to my next career.

"After I quit my practice, I soon became affiliated with the county coroner's office. The coroner was a friend of mine. There was a small stipend for case work. Actually, if you'd figured out how many hours I spent on a case and what I got paid, I might as well have been flipping hamburgers.

"What interested me in forensics was the challenges—trying to figure out the causes of death. In the past nine years I've been at over 1,000 autopsies. I'm continually taking courses, such as ballistics at the FBI and state police academies—these courses are so interesting.

"I've earned my credentials. I'm now Chief Deputy Coroner and a member of the state coroner's association. I also have a federal position with the National Disaster Services of the Department of Health and Human Services. I'm on 24-hour call for any disaster that might happen in my region.

"From time to time I may get special assignments. For example, during the 2000 Republican National Convention, I was the point man to make sure that body identification would be handled properly in case of any disaster. For seven days I lived on a military base, and driving to and from the base I had an unmarked white Suburban with tinted windows. I could park anywhere I wanted to. At the convention, I had a badge which gave me the same access rights as the FBI.

"I enjoy writing about forensics. I don't have to do it—I write just because I want the mental stimulation. I've had one paper published in an international journal, one by the Academy of Forensic Sciences, and I'm working on another.

"I could run for coroner and then I'd have a paid position. But I don't want to be tied down. I still want to take my vacations when I want to and do other things that interest me."

What advice would Norm give to a person who's thinking of starting the next career?

"It's not like it used to be. When you reached 65 you were dead. Now we have such a life expectancy that you have to continue living. Get out of your profession. You have to do something else.

"A productive person must keep being productive mentally and physically. If you just sit around and read books and watch television, you'll go out of your mind. Find something that you're interested in. No matter what it is, do it. Use your mind. Get yourself a basic schedule and stick to it."

What does Norm see as the effects of his new life?

"People tell me that I look younger now than I did ten years ago. I believe the reason why I do look younger is because I'm doing things I enjoy doing. . . . I wish I had more time. I feel that I have so much to offer to society that I just can't sit home on my butt."

Mark B.

Mark was a senior executive at a major publishing company. His company reorganized and Mark, then 57, lost his job. He received some job offers but decided that it was his time to play.

And play he did. Skiing. Tennis. Scuba diving. Sailing. Biking in France. Summers at his Cape Cod home. But after two years of this, Mark became increasingly dissatisfied. The "good life" seemed empty.

His wife suggested that he contact Habitat for Humanity, since Mark had skills that could be useful to that organization. While in college he had done part-time construction jobs, and before his publishing career he had worked for a construction company and helped supervise building projects.

Two days after Mark called the local Habitat branch, he was on the job. Mark enjoyed spending several days a week building homes. Soon, however, Mark was appointed to the board of directors and put in charge of the building committee. Mark now spends most of his time on board assignments, for which his experience as an executive has well prepared him.

What does Mark think about his volunteer work for Habitat? He claims there's "nothing like" watching people move into their own homes and seeing neighborhoods improve. Although Mark found his volunteer niche right away, he recommends that people join several groups to see which ones best meet their objectives.

Al F.

Formerly the international sales manager for Corning, Al "retired" at the age of 62. However, taking it easy was not an option for Al.

For one thing, he had always been active in community affairs: serving on the school board and church council, singing in the church choir, acting as a Little League director and a small-fry football coach. After leaving Corning, Al continued this kind of community work.

Soon, too, he began a new career—in politics. He was well prepared for politics because of his long-time involvement in community affairs. He was elected to the Corning city council, and then, after seven years, he was elected mayor, a position with many responsibilities but only a small stipend.

What does Al think about serving his community? Al has a plaque on his desk that states: "The only certain happiness in life is when you live your life for others."

Don C.

Don was 55 when he left his job as executive director of an area YMCA. Although there were parts of this job he enjoyed, he wanted to get out of daily administration and become more directly involved in community affairs. Since Don had grown up in an economically underprivileged area, he particularly wanted to help people in such localities become home owners.

Don was well equipped for such a project. He had served as an unpaid county commissioner for thirteen years, dealing with all levels of government. Knowing the difficulties caused by red tape, he wanted to work on small local projects where he could become involved from the start and make things happen fast.

As he put it, "If I get involved from the beginning I have greater commitment and sense of pride than if the projects are already underway. Besides, if they're local projects, you get to continually see the fruits of your labor."

Working with a community council of churches, Don helped found a nonprofit organization called Phoenixville Homes, of which he is now president. One of its offshoots is Home Ownership Phoenixville Encourages (HOPE).

After five years, HOPE has built or remodeled 25 homes. This is Don's favorite project. "When you turn over the keys to a family and they say, 'Thank you. Thank you. God bless you,' it's such a great feeling."

Some of the other projects connected with HOPE and Phoenixville Homes are these:

- The Flag House, a factory converted into 57 housing units for seniors.
- Community Home Ownership Repair Effort, or CHORE, which helps seniors who are homeowners but can't afford necessary repairs.
- Freedom House, a government-subsidized project that will provide 18 units for people with disabilities.
- The Good Samaritan Shelter for homeless men.

Now 67, Don is also president of Phoenixville Progressive Club, an organization of minority couples. One of this group's objectives is to encourage people of minority backgrounds to join and become leaders in community civic and religious organizations.

Don sums up his life changes in this way:

"I loved the YMCA and thank God that I had the opportunity to serve the community through the Y. However, if I had it to do all over again, I'd start my 'new life' quicker. I like to get my hands on something and make it happen. Sometimes I get a little too anxious and have to slow myself down.

"The feeling you get from helping others can't be measured in dollars and cents. I like to reach down and pull somebody up. I tell them that they don't owe me anything, just help somebody else. . . . Lift people up. That's what it's all about."

Dr. Bill S.

A number of years ago, when Dr. Bill thought of quitting his practice, his plans were to travel, paint, and play some golf. But it didn't turn out that way.

Back in 1988, the Samaritan House, a community organization that assisted underprivileged and homeless people, also wanted to also offer free medical care. Dr. Bill, an internist, volunteered his services, working one evening a week. Sensing the need, he gradually expanded his services to two nights a week.

In 1994 he quit his practice, but not just to travel, paint, and golf. Rather, it was to expand his work at the Samaritan House. About that time he also founded the Samaritan House Clinic, an offshoot of the Samaritan House.

Today the clinic has over 40 volunteers, including doctors, dentists, and pharmacists. They care for over 5,000 people a year. Doctors (usually over 50 years of age) frequently call to volunteer their services.

At the clinic, more holistic care can be given than in private practices. Dr. Bill, now 69, claims: "In private practice I used to get 15, 20 minutes, tops, with a new patient. Here we can take up to two hours."

The benefits of holistic care are twofold. First, patients get better treatment. For example, one of the patients had pains in his neck and back. In many practices, doctors would prescribe a muscle relaxant and move on to the next patient. But more than "normal" time with this patient revealed that his problem stemmed from sleeping in his home—which was a car. The parent organization, the Samaritan House, was able to find him shelter.

The medical givers also share in the benefits. In practicing medicine this way, Dr. Bill claims, "We are having more fun than we have a right to."

Bobby P.

Bobby P. started planning for his new career and testing it early, and he reaped the benefit. By the time he left his job, he had been preparing his new career for 14 years.

A violinist in the Philadelphia Orchestra, Bobby loved his job so much that sometimes he'd look around the stage and think, "I can't believe I'm getting paid to do this." Still, in 1997, at the age of 67, he felt it was time to leave. His new career beckoned.

He and his wife, Ellen F., had always wanted to give something back to the community that had supported Bobby during his career. Bobby thought it important that he continue his musical work. His wife had expertise in running nonprofit groups. Opening a nonprofit music school seemed like a natural extension of their expertise.

In 1983 Bobby and Ellen bought an old mansion and started their school on a small scale. Fourteen years later, when Bobby left the Philadelphia Orchestra, their school was up and running. In fact, their school had already run free programs for thousands of children, many of them students with disabilities or children from Philadelphia's economically underprivileged neighborhoods.

In May 2000 Bobby again took the stage of the Academy of Music, where he'd performed for 30 years. On this occasion it was Bobby's students who took the bow. Proud parents filled the audience. How did Bobby feel? "I miss performing, of course. But this? It's even better."

Herbert "Herb" H.

When Herb sold his executive search firm, he moved to Durham, North Carolina, a pleasant place to live. But he didn't want to "sit."

From Duke University's gerontologists he learned that aging is often accompanied by loneliness, which can lead to physical illness and depression. Herb thought that if older people could learn to use computers, there would be many ways for them to keep in touch with others.

At the time, Herb's computer knowledge was limited to rudimentary essentials, such as using e-mail and navigating the Web, so his first task was to develop additional computer skills. He then teamed up with a Methodist retirement home in Durham, donated three computers, and began teaching. His students learned how to use the computers to enhance their social lives.

Of the 16 people who enrolled in the program, 14 finished. Some used the Internet to play bridge. Others found companionship in chat rooms. A 69-year-old met a 71-year-old over the Internet, and soon they became engaged.

Herb's next project was with the Durham Jewish Family Service. Believing that computers intimidate many older people, he decided to help them learn to use Web TV.

Herb's mission to teach computer literacy does not stop with the elderly. He also works with elementary school children, showing them how to use the Internet.

Some Thoughts to Consider

Do you have a specific cause you'd like to advance?

For example, you may feel like Don, who wants to improve housing for those who need assistance, or Harold, who wants to help young children get off on the right track.

If you can't find a fit with a nonprofit organization, consider starting your own, as did Bobby and his wife. Your nonprofit might even be an informal, unstructured, one-person organization, such as Herb's.

You might work with others to form a nonprofit to carry out your mission, as Don did. Or set up an organization under the umbrella of a parent nonprofit organization, like Dr. Bill.

On the other hand, perhaps you don't yet have a specific cause you'd like to promote, but you'd like to use your skills to make this a better world, like Mark B. (Habitat). In that case, there's good news and bad news. The good news is that the United States has an estimated 175,000 nonprofits, and most of them are looking for volunteers. The bad news is that it might take time to find the one that's right for you. Although most nonprofits are looking for volunteers, in most cases it's for answering telephones, stuffing envelopes, and making cold-calls for donations. For help in finding the nonprofit that suits you, check Appendices A and B.

If you should choose a career of volunteering your services, you just might wind up thinking like Don, who says, "The feeling you get from helping others can't be measured in dollars and cents."

Decided on a Career Path? Undecided?

Perhaps you've decided on a career path. If so, take action to make that career a reality. Move on to Step 5.

But don't be discouraged if none of the career paths described here seems exactly right for you. You can find *that* career.

Don't let negative thoughts block out possibilities. Lloyd D., the former dean and college professor, claims: "I think the reason many of us don't break out of retirement is because of the fear of failure. It has been present all of our lives and is still there. We have lived with it so long we cannot shake it, even though we have fewer family obligations, financial worries, and less stake in our professions."

Remember: If you fail, so what? You can always try something else.

And as Theodore Roosevelt stated: "The credit goes to the man . . . who strives valiantly . . . his place shall never be with those whose cold and timid souls knew neither victory or defeat."

While going about your search, get involved with other people and with your community. You may discover that the opportunity finds you. Recall Fred M., the former CEO of an automobile parts trucking company, whom you met in the Introduction. "I became involved in a number of community projects," Fred says. "Through these programs I became friendly with a person who was also a SCORE district manager. He told me about SCORE: how it helped small businesses through counseling; how SCORE put its counselors through a training program to develop counseling skills; the comradeship of the counselors and things like that."

That sold Fred. He started doing volunteer work for SCORE. As you'll remember, it was here that Fred found his "why."

So, like Fred, don't hide yourself away. Get out there and meet people and investigate possibilities.

Take positive steps—today. Even if *that* career is still an unknown, start spending your time the way you want to—so much time for your career (the search), for your family, for your hobbies—all of the categories that are important to you. Do what you want to do.

Yes, you can start your renaissance today. Step 5 will show you how.

The Plan

Make Your Renaissance a Reality

During your previous career your routine may have been similar to Tom W.'s. Tom, as you'll recall, was formerly the vice president of sales for a computer software company.

Tom's typical work week, including commuting, was about 60 to 70 hours. He'd get home about 7 P.M. unless—as usually happened once or twice a week—he had a business dinner, in which case he'd arrive much later. On a normal night, after dinner with his wife, Pat, he'd make some phone calls to customers and staff, schedule the next day, shower, and then head off to bed.

Weekends were, as Tom put it, "recluse times." On Saturdays he'd run a few errands, do some household maintenance, catch up on paperwork. In the evenings, he and Pat might watch TV or go to a movie. Sundays he'd go to church, read the newspapers and trade journals, watch some TV, line up the upcoming week. Perhaps he'd also make some business telephone calls.

Like Tom, you may not have needed to give much thought to ways of spending your discretionary time. There wasn't much time to be discretionary about. But now the orders of the day are gone. Your pie chart is blank!

Earlier, in Step 3, you allocated your discretionary time—certain percentages for your career, family, hobbies. Now, though, you have to beware of losing sight of those good intentions. Without structure, two syndromes, the "What To

Do" and the "Time Trap," operating singly or in unison, may begin to govern your day-to-day affairs.

On some days you'll find yourself with seemingly nothing to do. Free-floating anxiety sets in. You lie down on the couch and half-watch TV. Soon you start fretting about your kids, your significant other, your stock portfolio, the economy—you name it. This is the "What To Do" syndrome.

Or, unfettered by a schedule, your time may be filled with countless small time-wasters. You sleep later than you normally would. You read the newspapers—and do you ever read newspapers! You turn on the TV to check the news, weather, or stock market: You become transfixed, so you watch for an hour or so. You've fallen prey to the "Time Trap" syndrome.

If you truly enjoy spending your days this way, fine. But most likely you'll find yourself thinking, "My time just disappears. I'm not getting anything done." And your renaissance will just be a dream.

Don't waste your most valuable resource—time.

Plan.

And put your plan in writing.

Now this is a stopper for many people. "*In writing?* Why not just think it through? After all, we're not talking about planning for Microsoft."

Sure, you can benefit from just thinking about your plan. But you know that a written plan has advantages. Writing is a tough discipline. Often our thoughts seem crystal clear until we write them out; then we find gaps and inconsistencies—plus many problems we never considered. Besides, if your plan is documented, it'll be in sharper focus. Your commitment will be stronger and more lasting; old ways will be less likely to resurface.

Sketching out your plan needn't take much time. The document doesn't have to be lengthy or elegant. All that's necessary is that you can understand your plan when you refer to it.

You likely have experience—possibly considerable experience—in planning. You will notice that this step follows commonly accepted planning procedures, except that they have been greatly simplified and adapted to lifestyle planning. Consider much of this step, then, as review.

Here we'll cover four major aspects of planning: Charting Your Course; Scheduling Your Activities; Monitoring Your Course; and Revising Your Course, When Necessary.

Charting Your Course

You've decided how you want allocate your time. (If you haven't already determined how much time you'd like to allocate to your career, family, friends, and so forth, why not do so now? You can find a form and instructions in Step 3, pp. 40–42.) Now, to determine specifically what you'd like to do during these time periods, develop a master plan.

Include in your Master Plan three types of plans—referred to here as *descriptive, sequenced,* and *contingency.*

Descriptive Plans

For some of your categories, all you'll need will be a notation of the time allocation and a one-line statement that describes the activity. For example, if you allocate 10 hours a week to managing your investments, what activities (action plans) do you plan to accomplish during these 10 hours? A simple note will be enough.

For some categories, even describing the activities isn't necessary. Take the category "Hobbies." Ask Doug, the food broker, what hobby he'd like to pursue, and he'll immediately answer, "Golf." Ask Dr. Walter, the chief of obstetrics and gynecology, and he'll say, "My farm." At this stage in the planning process, providing more detail for Doug's golf and Dr. Walter's farm activities would be useless—the type of planning you've probably detested and tried to avoid throughout your working life.

Another category where you might use one-line statements is time with friends. The descriptive statement might simply be, "Time with friends," plus the number of hours you have allocated for this category.

But watch out for oversimplification. For instance, when it comes right down to it, you may be short of ideas for activities for "Time with friends." It may seem that all you ever do is go out to dinner. Sure, you have fun. Still, you'd still like to do new, different things with your friends. But what?

Do the obvious. Consider putting together lists of possible activities, and from time to time add to these inventories of ideas. Since compiling lists is something we tend to keep putting off, set target dates for completing your lists.

Sequenced Plans

You may have some categories that involve a number of activities—some that must be done in sequence.

Suppose you're considering moving from the East Coast to the Southwest and starting a new career—renovating houses. You want to make a month-long exploratory trip to check out the area.

Before you leave home, you should do background work, like deciding on the kind of area where you'd like to live and work; finding areas that meet those criteria; selecting the areas you want to visit first, second, and so forth; determining the type—price, condition, neighborhood—of homes you'd like to renovate; making contacts with realtors; and possibly reading a few books on renovating houses.

Since these preparatory activities are mostly new to you, it'll probably pay to put such "to do" tasks in sequence, along with estimated time requirements and completion dates.

Contingency Plans

J. Paul Getty, who was one of the richest—and some would say, luckiest—men on earth, once said, "When I go into any business deal, my chief thoughts are how I'm going to save myself when things go wrong."

Some years ago a study was made of lucky people—not people who happened to hit the lottery once, but people who tended to be lucky throughout their lives. Lucky people are generally happy, but they're also pessimistic. They always seem to be planning what they will do in the event of a disaster.

On the other hand, chronic losers seem to be plagued with large doses of over-optimism. Just watch people hemorrhaging tons of money at gaming tables. They're extremely optimistic.

Before you finish this stage of planning, look over your plans. Are any, in some way, putting you at risk? If so, consider having contingency plans in case these at-risk situations become realities. For example:

WHEN YOU ARE STARTING A BUSINESS IN AN UNFAMILIAR FIELD. Starting any new business is risky. Starting one that is unfamiliar to you can produce all the usual perils, and a couple you've never dreamed of. Obviously, you'll research the stuffing out of the new business. And you may also want to start out conservatively.

Perhaps you can take a cue from Ken, who now runs a specialty hardware store. When he first opened his business, he continued his regular job. He ran his shop by hiring employees and working evenings. That way, if his venture turned out to be unsuccessful, he could continue at his old job. As it happened, Ken never needed to put his contingency plan into action, but having such a plan certainly helped to ease his tensions.

WHEN LOSSES MIGHT SERIOUSLY AFFECT YOUR FINANCIAL SITUA-
TION. Some new career paths may require substantial up-front
investments. If the outlay might jeopardize your financial security, plan accordingly. Build in flexibility.

For instance, if you're starting a new business, maybe you
can lease facilities instead of buying. Maybe you can subcon-
tract operations rather than doing them in-house. Such options
allow you a quicker escape from an unpromising situation.

You may want to start small, even if finances aren't a problem. As you learn the ropes, you'll probably have to make
changes and adjustments. These adaptations are much easier if
the scale of your operation is small. Don, the custom furniture
manufacturer, started out as a one-person operation. It was
only after his business was successful that he added personnel.

WHEN MOVING TO A NEW LOCATION. If changing your resi-
dence is part of your plan, can you position the move as an ex-
periment? There are many reasons why you might want to go
back home—for instance, to be near your children, grandchildren, or other relatives and friends.

In many cases, you don't have to burn your bridges. For example, you could rent in the new location for a year. If it turns
out that you like your life there, then you can make the change
permanent.

The following page has a worksheet that will help you
make a simple record of your Master Plan. (For a set of Master
Plan Worksheets, detailed instructions, and an explanatory
case example, see Appendix C, pp. 173–176, 191–196.)

Scheduling Your Activities

Dr. Richard, the psychiatrist, after reviewing an early draft of
this book, had this to say: "I'm going to start scheduling my
time. I just realized how much time I'm wasting."

Master Plan Worksheet

Activity	Time Allocation	Action Plan	Completion Date

From the outset, schedule your activities and stick to that schedule. Even if you don't fall victim to the "What to Do" or "Time Trap" syndromes, for one reason or another, some categories will probably be neglected.

You may spend too large a chunk of time on your career, as you may have done for most of your life. Perhaps you've already made a career decision, and you'll focus too heavily on getting your new venture up and moving, thinking, "Once I get established, I'll have time for friends and vacations."

There's never an end to this pattern: "Once I hire an assistant...." "Once I move out of my house into an office...." "Once I get my distribution channel in order...." Even if you haven't decided on a career yet, you may be overzealous in your search.

Or maybe it won't be your career that usurps too much of your time. You may get on a roll doing something else—reading, fishing, golfing. The result? Time with family, time with friends, time for self-improvement—things you always wanted to do—get sidelined.

Scheduling is just as important in your new life as it was in your old one. And you can go about it in pretty much the same way. However, there is one major difference: In your previous life, you most likely scheduled only appointments, meetings, social affairs, and such; now you'll be scheduling all of your discretionary time. As we've seen, this will amount to somewhere between 80 and 110 hours per week.

Schedule these hours fairly strictly for at least the first several months. Programming all of your discretionary time will become less important once your new lifestyle becomes second nature.

See the next two pages for a sample Weekly Scheduling Worksheet. (For a set of Weekly Scheduling Worksheets, detailed instructions, and an explanatory case example, see Appendix C, pp. 174–181, 197–202.)

Weekly Scheduling Worksheet (Week of _________)

Time	Sunday	Monday	Tuesday
6–7 A.M.			
7–8			
8–9			
9–10			
10–11			
11–12			
12–1 P.M.			
1–2			
2–3			
3–4			
4–5			
5–6			
6–7			
7–8			
8–9			
9–10			
10–11			
11–12			

Weekly Scheduling Worksheet *(continued)*

Wednesday	Thursday	Friday	Saturday

Monitoring Your Course

You have a bout with the flu. You're called for jury duty. Some kid rear-ends your car.

Some disruptions you can prevent. Others, like jury duty and when that kid rear-ends you, well, you can't.

Whether avoidable or not, you know this for sure: Disruptions are a way of life, and they'll wreak havoc with your planned activities and time allocations.

Even during those rare times when you've had a week miraculously free of calamitous events, you're still likely to stray from your schedule. "Bad" habits have a way of recurring—or developing—without your notice.

Lloyd, the former dean and business professor, commented: "I think you'll find that you're spending more time than you'd like on activities such as reading the newspapers, checking everything on the computer, watching pro football games. Without analyzing how you're spending your time, you're possibly likely to be frustrated and unhappy and won't know why. I think this is true for me."

Regardless of what throws you off schedule, you can optimize the way you spend your time. Start by using the Time Analysis Worksheet—it will help you analyze how you actually spend your time in relation to your planned schedule.

See the following page for a sample Time Analysis Worksheet. (For a set of Time Analysis Worksheets and detailed instructions, see Appendix C, pp. 179–186.)

Revising Your Course, When Necessary

As a general rule, don't make major changes in your Master Plan during the first few weeks. Even if your actual time expenditures are so far from your planned schedule that you're tempted to chuck the whole process, stay with your original plan for at least four weeks.

Time Analysis Worksheet

Activity	Time Allocated	Time Spent				
		Week 1	Week 2	Week 3	Week 4	Total
Career						
Family						
Religion						
Volunteer work						
Existing friends						
New friends						
Clubs, associations						
Investments						
Physical fitness						
Self-improvement						
Errands, doctor visits, etc.						
Avocations, hobbies						
Other						
Total						

For one thing, you'll get better at scheduling and sticking to your schedules. For another, a week or two is really not enough time to tell you anything concrete about your character or your preferences. Give yourself time to find out what you really enjoy and what you're really willing to do.

After a month, compare the time that you actually spent with the time you allocated for each category. It's likely you'll find variations. Of course, you may have gotten off track through no fault of your own—a family emergency, a period of bad weather—but usually the discrepancies tell you something important about your schedule and yourself. You probably need to take action.

You may have to make major changes in your time allocations. You may realize you've overlooked a category that you should have allocated time for. (Look at Humberto C.'s time allocations on p. 40. When does he intend to run his errands?)

Then there's a good possibility that you've underestimated the time needed for sleeping, showering, shaving, and so forth. You may not actually have as much discretionary time as you think. (I found out that about 85 hours, not 100, was right for me.)

You may have to change some of the activities you listed. It's important to stay flexible enough to recognize what gives you a zest for living. If an activity that looked good on paper doesn't feel that way in practice, you'll want to avoid it. Perhaps it's one that really excited you when you could squeeze in only an hour or two a month, but once you started spending 20 hours a week at it, you became bored.

It may turn out that you need to reassess your lifestyle. Armed with your new insights, you'll be better positioned this time to find your true renaissance. Remember Warren O., the trail guide publisher? When he left his government position, he opened a specialty footwear retailing shop in Maryland. But Warren soon realized this was not his passion. Instead of slogging through a joyless career, he moved to where he wanted to be and did what he wanted to do.

But the problem could also be self-discipline or time use. Perhaps you've kept finding excuses not to put in your hour of exercising every other day. The "need" to spend more time with *The Wall Street Journal* has suddenly taken the place of the treadmill.

If you've been procrastinating on something that really must be done—like exercising or spending time with family—you need to face up to your delaying tactics and try to do better.

Get Your Pencil

The particular method of planning for your renaissance is not all-important. What is critical is that you know how you want to spend your time and actually spend it that way.

If you decide to use the method I recommend, you can chart your course and schedule your next week's activities in less than two hours. You already have everything you need in front of you, except a pencil. Extra forms appear on pp. 175–176 and 180–183 in Appendix C. Make copies—or enlargements—of these forms if you like. Or grab a ruler and paper and make up your own forms—it's easy to do.

If you need help in filling out the forms, Appendix C has instructions for each set of forms, along with a case example.

Regardless of whether you use my method or some other one, start your renaissance today. Don't just run out of time.

Once you're underway, it's important to give your renaissance the credit it merits. And the next step will show you how.

The Communication

Give Your Renaissance the Standing It Deserves

"A rose by any other name smells the same." Right?

Wrong.

Just ask the Coke executives at Atlanta who are still smarting over the New Coke flop. Blind taste tests showed that New Coke tasted better than the old Coke. Yet, once on the market, it was thumbs down for New Coke. Why? The old Coke, in its familiar packaging, just tasted better.

Perception is reality.

How will professional acquaintances, friends, relatives, and others perceive your renaissance career? Think especially about how they will react if your career involves:

- ➤ Continuing to work for your present company, or another firm, on a reduced-time schedule or as a part-time consultant
- ➤ Scaling down your present business
- ➤ Starting a new business, perhaps one where you're the only employee and you are working out of your home
- ➤ Starting an artistic career—for instance, as a writer, artist, or actor
- ➤ Working as a volunteer for a nonprofit

The way you present your career will govern the way it's perceived. Do it right and people will see you as enthusiastic and adventuresome. Do it wrong and others will believe you're an "R" person.

Of course, there are those who scoff, "Why should I care what others think of my career?" Yet these same people spend big bucks on homes, cars, and clothing, intended, at least in part, to impress others. Should you place your life's mission in a less favorable light than your shoes?

Even more critical is how you communicate your career to yourself. Do it wrong and you'll lose self-respect and confidence in your new career. The "why" will fade. Your career will propel you to your renaissance only if you wholeheartedly believe that it is one that makes a difference, that somehow you're making a contribution. And the more importance you attach to your career, the greater the propellant.

Here are six suggestions to give your career the standing it deserves:

1. Banish the "R" Words

We talked briefly about this before, but now let's put the matter in a broader context. If you're used to spending 60 hours a week on the job and now you're spending only 30, you may feel you're a semi-"R" person. Or that your new work is a "retirement career." Well, wipe out those thoughts—in a hurry!

Using the "R" words in describing your new career will bring up inferences of "withdrawing," "retreating," and "discarded" to others and even to yourself.

Think of a CEO of a major corporation who finds time for work with charitable organizations, for mountain climbing, and for yacht racing. Imagine this person describing himself or herself as "semi-retired" to the board of directors!

As ridiculous as this seems, some very active people use "semi-retired" without careful thought about how it may be perceived by others. John S., for example, is in his late 50s. He has a Ph.D. in marketing. Once a college professor, he now has a small marketing research firm. He'd like to build up his business, and ideally, make it a desirable acquisition candidate.

Yet he refers to himself as "semi-retired."

Do clients want someone who is half-withdrawn, half-retreating, and half-discarded to spearhead fact-finding that's vital to their firms' growth—and perhaps even survival? No wonder John's business isn't growing very fast.

Also avoid the phrase "retirement career." You've seen books and articles about "retirement careers." And you've heard people use that phrase when they talk about careers. So isn't it a positive term? Maybe old codgers think so, but younger people don't. Nor, as we've seen, do the dictionaries.

No "R" words in talking about your new career!

2. Don't Mention Your Previous Career

You may be proud of your former career. In order to give yourself more credibility, you may think, "Why not refer to my former position?"

Be careful. That approach could backfire, as it did for me.

My wife and I were vacationing in southern France. I had just quit my job, but my official resignation wouldn't take place for another six weeks. At that time I would start my new career.

We were having lunch in a sidewalk cafe. A French businessman, sitting next to us, overheard us pondering the meaning of a French word. He volunteered the definition. This started a conversation, and we invited him to join us.

The three of us got around to asking each other about our professions. He was a salesman. "What do you do?" he asked.

I thought a university professor would have more status than a start-up career counselor, so I said, "Right now I'm a university professor, but I'm starting a new occupation as a career counselor."

He studied me for a moment and then said (with a French accent), "Oh, you're retiring."

3. Have Business Cards and Stationery

If you're working for a large organization, you'll probably get the supporting materials you need for a transition to your new career. But if you're on your own, you'll have to put together these resources. There are two tools that are essential: business cards and stationery.

If you're starting a career as a self-employed artist or writer, or possibly your own start-up company that won't be operational for some time, you may think, "Why should I have business cards or stationery now?"

Put away that thought. Business cards and stationery will help convince others that you mean business. They will also make your career seem more real and important to you.

And while you're having them made, spend a few extra dollars. Think how often you've rubbed business cards (and even stationery) between your thumb and index finger to see whether they were embossed.

Simplistic advice? Sure. Important? You bet!

4. Prepare an Articulate Career Description

When you're asked "What do you do?" make sure your response is articulate and convincing.

If You're Searching for That *Career*

You've got a ready-made answer. Jut mention your relevant key search descriptors. For example, Pete (p. 188) might say, "I'm interested in starting some type of for-profit business—

preferably in building and construction—doing something where I can be creative, set goals, and initiate projects. I'd like to live somewhere in the Southwest. Oh, not in a border town, but in a place that's more crime-free. And I'd like to do some traveling and have adventure."

Besides keeping you from being pigeon-holed with "R" people, you might get some ideas which will lead you to *that* career.

If You've Decided on a Career

In some cases—if you're writing a novel, for example—your business card may say it all.

But in other instances, such as opening a one-person business or volunteering for a nonprofit, consider scripting a short sound bite.

In an ordinary conversation, 20 seconds is about all the time you'll have for an answer, and that's all the time it should take.

Suppose you've decided to follow a career of doing volunteer work for SCORE. Here's an example of a 20-second description you could use.

Job description and affiliation:
"I'm a management counselor, affiliated with SCORE."

Target market:
"Our target market is small business firms. We work in conjunction with the Small Business Association."

Service:
"We provide advisory assistance to our clients, such as helping them develop their business plans."

That's about as much as you can say in 20 seconds. In case people would like to hear more, have another concise answer that expands the description of the target market and the services you offer.

Beyond your career description, also prepare answers to two questions that you'll be asked about your new career: "What are your qualifications?" and "Why are you interested in this field?"

If you're starting a career where you're inexperienced, expect another question: "Why did you decide on this?"

Know what you're going to say.

5. Broadcast Your Career Change

When you're starting your new career, you may feel uneasy, as I did, about meeting certain people. You can't fall back on the status or reputation of your previous career.

A good career description can cast a positive light on your new career. Even so, how will your career change appear to others? To your friends? To casual business and social acquaintances? Will it appear that you're taking a step down from your previous job? Will your career look like the dabbling of a semi-"R" person? Or, even worse, like merely a front?

So how should you announce your career change? As soon and as positively as possible.

You know that business reputations are, to a great degree, built by word of mouth. In your new career, the first words, and the first mouth, will be your own. So do right by yourself.

For example, when I had just quit my job and begun my start-up career, I was operating out of my home. My business phone was the same as my home phone, and I had no employees.

I was almost 72 years old. I could just imagine what people might think when I told them about my new career: Their eyes would glaze over. They'd be thinking the "R" words.

I had particularly dreaded going to a board meeting of a charitable organization. There were a number of influential men and women on the board. I was certain that my stature as a university professor had played a major role in my appoint-ment to that board.

When they found out about my career change, would they associate me with the "R" words? There was a good chance, especially since I was about seven years older than anyone else.

When I arrived, someone said, "Hello, Professor."

Knowing they would find out sooner or later, I decided sooner would be better. "Ex-professor," I said. "I'm starting a new business."

One asked, "What is it?"

"Career counseling. Our target market is people between 55 and 75 who are financially secure and have had successful business careers. We plan to provide our clients with struc-tured counseling to help them focus their energies on finding that 'why' they must live for."

One of the members asked me to explain more of what we did, so I expanded a bit. Much to my surprise—and delight—the chair of the board told me that he had retired early be-cause he wanted more time to play golf, vacation, and just en-joy life. He went on to say, "But you can only play so much golf. I really went through a crisis. I decided I had to do some-thing more meaningful. That's why I got involved with a start-up company and began doing work like this."

He then added, "Bob, once you get underway, I've got a number of friends I've got to put you in touch with. They re-ally need help."

Another board member mentioned that ten years before he had been CEO of a billion-dollar company but decided that the job wasn't worth it. So he quit and started a one-man con-sulting business. "I've never been happier. Bob, if you weren't excited about what you were doing, you did the right thing."

I found support among the board members for my new vo-cation, and at the same time began building my client base.

6. Don't Overpromise

Talk in a positive, enthusiastic, realistic way. Believe what you say, and then make it come true.

Getting started on your new career may take longer than you think, especially if you're changing your occupation or switching industries.

Don't tell everyone that you'll finish your book, get your business established—or whatever—in six months, when if everything doesn't go right it'll take much longer. People will continually ask how you're coming along. You'll find it discomforting to tell them that you're behind—way behind—schedule. After a while they may view your career as sort of quixotic.

A Brief Recap

Remember the quote from Nietzsche mentioned in Step 1? "He who has the why to live can bear almost any how." This brings us back to where we started.

The *why*—which you define for yourself—is that *something* you live for. Knowing your *why*—and planning to achieve it—will let you indulge and enjoy life in the deepest way possible.

Life should be an adventure, an expedition, whose day-to-day tasks give pleasure. And what could give you greater pleasure than spending your days seeking the life you truly want? The thrill is in the journey, not in the achievement.

If you're wholeheartedly working at, or trying to find, *that* career, and if you've made a sincere commitment to jump-start other aspects of your life, you already have a new beginning.

Yes, you have your rebirth, your renaissance.

Epilogue

Remember when you were a kid and the circus came to town? You wanted *the* best spot to watch the parade. You got there hours early.

Finally—off in the distance—you could see the brightly plumed drum major. And then the band wagon was right in front of you. Then came the bearded woman, the strong man rippling his muscles, tigers growling and pacing in their cages, the bulb-nosed, baggy-suited clowns—and one of them reached over and rubbed your head.

Yes, you had the best possible spot.

But all too soon, all you could see were the rears of elephants waddling off in the distance. The parade had moved on.

When you find your renaissance, it's like finding that one best spot for the parade. The problem is that the parade of life keeps moving.

Ben Franklin said that two things in life were certain: death and taxes. He was only two-thirds right. He should have added another certainty: *change.*

So a renaissance is not like winning the big prize once and forever. It's winning the right to keep playing. It means a continual rebirth, replacing the old with the new. You have to keep adapting. And that means possible changes in both your career and other aspects of your life.

To stay with the parade, place yourself in situations that will foster adaptive thinking. Surround yourself with people who are doing exciting things, who have a zest for living, who, directly or indirectly, can help you capitalize on the new world.

Don't get cocooned in a small, exclusive circle of friends. John, the COO of a start-up firm, had this to say: "I have a lot of very close friends. But if I spent all my time with them, I'd lack the stimulation that I get from being bombarded by different perspectives from people of different ages, different cultures and races."

Seek out new, stimulating activities. Take exotic trips with ElderTreks, host foreign visitors, be a mentor to school children, study at the Chautauqua Institute. Join a book group or a "great decisions" discussion group.

Take up yoga. Study French. Learn how to chicken dance or tango, how to become a clown, how to shoot skeet. Help the Salvation Army, participate in an archeology project, conduct research for the U.S. Geological Survey.

Attend an ecology camp, participate in a National Issues Forum, become involved in the theater. Go whitewater canoeing.

And make the most of today. Regardless of your age or health, it's the only day you can count on. That's the way it always has been, that's the way it always will be.

One of the greatest boxers of all time, Joe Louis, said it right, "You only live once, but if you live it right, once is enough."

Research Resources

Researching your career is like preparing a room for painting: scraping out the cracks, filling them with spackle, sanding. Not an exciting task, but essential.

As the long-time coach of Penn State's Nittany Lions, Joe Paterno, claims: "The will to win is important, but the will to prepare is vital."

Pages 107–108 tell the story of Jack A., who got involved in a gold-mining venture after retiring from the advertising business. Although this business was new to Jack, he couldn't refuse the opportunity to get back into the game. The business didn't pan out, so to speak. Jack was forced to shut it down, and he incurred a major financial loss.

In retrospect, it's obvious that Jack should have done his homework before digging himself into his new career. Time and again we read about new ventures that fail, and often the problem is that people didn't do thorough research ahead of time.

It may have been a while since you've been involved in research projects. Consequently, I've sorted out what I believe are the best ways to get the information you need, rather than giving you a huge compendium of sources that might lead to distraction and frustration.

This appendix contains descriptions of 14 research sources and tips on how to use them. The list of contents on the next page will help you find the section you need.

Appendix A Contents

Books

Visit a good-sized library or bookstore. If you can't locate what you want right away, find a knowledgeable librarian or bookstore clerk and ask for help.

If you haven't used the Internet for finding and ordering books, you'll be surprised at how easy it is. Direct your Web browser to sites such as Barnes & Noble <www.bn.com>, Borders <www.borders.com>, and Amazon <www.amazon.com>. You can search these sites by title, author, subject, or keywords.

The major online booksellers also provide price, publisher, publication date, and number of pages. For many books you'll find other information such as tables of contents, excerpts from the book, reader ratings and reviews, reviews by critics, and sometimes links to job-hunting Web sites and career advice.

Professional Journals, Magazines, Trade Publications, and Newspaper Articles

Use your local library's facilities. Most likely your library subscribes to an electronic database. If so, on the Internet you'll have access to abstracts or full-text articles from, in the case of EBSCOhost, almost 3,000 periodicals, about 150 newspapers, and six news wires, both current and archived.

Imagine you want to find out about a subject area, a person, or a company and your library subscribes to EBSCOhost. After you're on your library's Web site, look for a link to "Magazine and Newspaper Indexes" or something similar (titles will vary). Click on EBSCOhost. Most likely, you'll need to type in your library card barcode, and *voila!* You're presented with a space for typing in your request.

Most libraries will let you access EBSCOhost from any remote computer, even from your own home. Should you have problems in your search (mostly likely it'll be in narrowing your search), call the reference librarian.

If your library doesn't subscribe to an electronic database, talk with the research librarian. It's surprising how quickly that person can guide you to the information you'll need.

The Internet

Although you can find out about almost anything on the Internet, the first trick is navigating through the Web. The second is sorting the chaff from the informational grain. (If you feel you're not expert enough—or have no inclination—to do Internet searches, visit your local library. Usually libraries have staff that can provide assistance.)

For a handy guide to search techniques, go to the University of California at Berkeley's Web site, <www.lib.berkeley.edu/help/search.html>. If you're relatively inexperienced in searching the Internet, you may be better off getting a book; I recommend *The Internet for Dummies*, 8th Edition, (New York: John Wiley & Sons, 2002).

Following are ways you can gather information on the Internet for for-profit (employed), for-profit (self-employed), artistic (self-employed), and volunteer careers.

For-Profit (Employed) Careers

GENERAL. Probably your best bet is to check with an association in your field of interest using Weddle's Web site, <www.weddles.com/associations>. For example, the Direct Marketing Association, a link under the general heading of Marketing, has—among its many online resources—an events calendar (conferences, seminars, and chapters), a job bank, and partial access to its library.

If you'd like references for topics such as future trends, careers in high demand, details on specific careers, and ways to market yourself, take a look at CareerPlanner.com, <www.career-planning.com>.

COMPANY AND SALARY. You can find general information about a specific company by accessing the company's Web site. Type the company's name into a search engine to find the company's home page.

If you don't have the company's Web site, or if you're interested in finding out about a number of companies, check with your local library. Possibly the library subscribes to *Reference USA*. Updated monthly, this directory lists over 12 million businesses in its database, giving company names, phone numbers, addresses, type of business, sales, and number of employees. Most likely you can access this resource from home. And you can pinpoint your search. For example, if you're interested in a certain type of business, you can search by state, area code, zip code, county, and city.

For salary ranges, go to most any job-hunting Web site. Here you can find salary ranges by title of position, or an even more tailored evaluation of a particular job. For example, at Monster.com <www.monster.com>, the Career Advice section has a Salary Info page that computes the market evaluation based on occupation, field, and geographic location. Monster.com's Career Advice also has links to résumé tips, interviewing, and networking.

JOB OPENINGS. Consider putting your résumé on a job site on the Web. Resumes are quick and easy to post, and you can do it for free. Job sites will usually give you information on how to prepare your résumé.

Use a Web site that lists employment opportunities and automatically matches your résumé to relevant job openings (<www.monster.com> is my favorite site for this purpose). At many such sites, when matches are found, both you and the employers will be notified by e-mail. Employers may contact you or you can contact them.

Don't expect miraculous results. Only a small percentage of job seekers get their jobs via the Internet (4 percent, according to a Forrester Research study in 2000). Still, given its simplicity—and since it's cost free—posting your résumé on the Internet is a tactic worth considering.

Besides job sites, check with an appropriate association. Weddle's site, <www.weddles.com/associations>, would be a good place to start.

Of course, sites and the technology are changing fast. When you begin serious job hunting, look for current articles that offer the lowdown on various job-hunting sites and Internet strategies. Or talk with a librarian.

For-Profit (Self-Employed) Careers

FINE-TUNING OR RIGHT-SIZING A BUSINESS. After you're on an online search engine, type in the phrase "fine-tuning and business and profitability" or the phrase "right-sizing and business and profitability." If the results don't meet your needs, refine your search. (Need ideas on how to narrow your search? Refer to <www.lib.berkeley.edu/TeachingLib/Guides/Internet/Strategies.html>. Or give your librarian a call.)

STARTING A BUSINESS. For a broad range of entrepreneurial topics, here are my top two recommendations:

- *U.S. Small Business Association* (my favorite) <www.sba.gov/starting_business>. This site is informative and easy to navigate. The topic areas include research, startup, business plans, workshops, seminars and courses, counseling help (SBA is affiliated with SCORE), shareware, and assets for sale. If you're interested in visiting other sites, the SBA site has links to more than 30.
- *AARP* <www.aarpsmallbiz.com>. Also easy to navigate, this site's links include access to capital, communications, human resources, legal resources, "my industry," "my office," a reference library, sales and marketing, taxes and accounting, and a technology center. The site also offers many other features that a person just starting a business would find useful, such as a free Internet course on how to start a business. There are also links to sites where you can get information on such topics as competitive tools, international import/export, and government resources.

Artistic (Self-Employed) Careers

Use an online search engine, such as <www.google.com>, to search for terms such as "freelance writing and career"; "photography and career"; and "becoming a poet." You'll probably get all the information you need—and then some. In fact, you'll probably have to refine your search.

Volunteer Careers

By typing "volunteer organizations" in an online search engine, you'll get a long list of Web sites, such as these:

- ➤ Idealist.org: <www.idealist.org>
- ➤ SERVEnet: <www.servenet.org>
- ➤ USA Freedom Corps: <www.freedomcorps.gov>
- ➤ VolunteerMatch: <www.volunteermatch.org> (Volunteer-Match claims to have made over 1,000,000 connections in its first four years.)

On some sites, if you specify your location and your volunteering interests, you'll be directed to relevant local agencies.

Perhaps locality isn't a constraint for you. Maybe you'd like to do volunteer work overseas. The Internet sources just mentioned can tell you about international organizations. (Also check p. 155 for a listing of organizations that act as a clearing-house for volunteers and nonprofit agencies.)

People Knowledgeable About Your Area of Interest

Some industries and methods of doing business are changing so rapidly that printed literature is often out of date. For specific "inside" facts about a career you're considering, your best source may be people who are directly involved.

You may, for instance, want information about:

- ➤ Required skills for a specific job
- ➤ Who your co-workers would be

➤ The competitive environment for a business venture you're considering

You may be able to get information from a company or organization. If you don't have inside contacts, see the person whose job it is to disseminate information. If this person can't help, ask to be referred to someone who can.

Networking

Once you can be specific about the nature of your search, cast your net wider. *Broadcast* your interests. Tell your relatives, close associates, accountant, dentist, doctor, insurance agent, and lawyer, as well as members of your clubs, your civic groups, and your religious congregation.

Also start a secondary-tier network. Ask whether your primary acquaintances have friends or associates you could contact.

Sometimes unexpected sources will lead you to that *something.* John H. heard that one of his son's friends was starting a company and needed someone to take charge of day-to-day operations. Fred got involved with SCORE because of casual conversations with a fellow member of a civic organization.

Follow the *ABC rule.* Even the most optimistic fishermen know that casting once and then dozing off is no way to catch a fish. A serious fisherman casts the line again and again, trying one spot in the stream, then another and another. Hence the ABC rule:

Always Be Casting.

When you talk to friends, let them know about your career interests and listen to their suggestions. When you meet someone new who might have useful information, find out as much as you can.

Associations

To locate an association in your field, go to your library and look in the *Encyclopedia of Associations*, published by the Gale Group. The three volumes list nearly 23,000 national and international organizations, divided into categories such as "educational," "cultural," "social welfare," "public affairs." "business," "governmental," "environmental," and "legal."

For example, if you're interested in artists and art associations, there are over 600 listed; photographers, over 200; theater actors, over 100; authors and publishers, over 300. Most public libraries subscribe to this valuable resource. The keyword lists and index will help you navigate through the thousands of associations to discover the ones that interest you.

For each association you'll find, among other information, its address, telephone and fax numbers, e-mail address, Web site, titles of publications, and number of staff and members. You can also learn the times and locations of its conventions or meetings.

Most associations have helpful publications, or at a minimum, staff or member officers you can talk to and find out more about the industry. Many larger associations, besides holding conventions, offer courses and seminars. Many publish employment opportunities and short bios of job applicants. Some also hold job fairs where employers and employees can meet (usually as part of the national meetings).

If you're interested in volunteer work, consider associations that act as job clearing-houses for opportunities (local, national, and international) and volunteers. They may be able to put you in touch with one or more organizations that can use your services. Among these associations are:

- ➤ AARP: 800-424-3410, <www.aarp.org>
- ➤ American Red Cross: 800-435-7669, <www.redcross.org>

- Catholic Network of Volunteer Services: 800-543-5046, <www.cnvs.org>
- Lutheran Volunteer Corps: 202-387-3222, <www.lvchome.org>
- Senior Corps: 800-424-8867, <www.seniorcorps.org>

Apprenticeships

If you need hands-on training—but not the kind you can get from an educational program or on the job—consider doing an apprenticeship. Here are several suggestions to help you find an organization willing to work with you.

- Make direct contact with an organization and simply ask. This is probably your best bet.
- Search the Web using the term *apprenticeship* combined with your skill interest.
- Contact an association related to your area of interest. To locate association addresses, check the *Encyclopedia of Associations*.

Consultants

For the career you have in mind, you may lack the necessary experience in operations, marketing, finance, or some other aspect. If so, think about bringing in outsiders who understand your business.

FREE COUNSELING. The Service Corps of Retired Executives (SCORE) has over 12,400 volunteer mentors to assist aspiring entrepreneurs and small business owners. SCORE provides free and confidential individual counseling, as well as low-cost workshops and seminars at the local chapter level (SCORE has about 400 chapters throughout the United States). E-mail counseling, available through SCORE's Web site at <www.score.org>, allows you to get free and confidential mentoring without leaving your home or place of business.

Besides its Web site, you can contact SCORE by calling its national office at 800-634-0245.

PAID CONSULTANTS. A hired gun will cost money, but if it's an important decision, the price you pay may be small. If you haven't dealt with consultants before, make sure that the consultant is an expert in your specific problem area. Also insist on references and make sure you understand all fee charges—time and expenses—before you make any agreement.

Municipal Agencies

Here are some suggestions to help you ferret out what's available in a certain community, or in a larger one nearby.

CHAMBER OF COMMERCE. Personnel in this office usually have a good grasp of what's available and going on in the community. Make this your first call, regardless of whether you're seeking information about seminars, workshops, local associations and companies, support groups, for-profit and volunteer job opportunities, or some other career data.

YOUR COMMUNITY WEB SITE. If the community has a Web site, check it out. Get the Internet address from the Chamber of Commerce.

AGENCY REFERRALS. Suppose you're thinking about a career in teenage drug and alcohol prevention. Call the board of education or the police force. Find out which volunteer organizations they consider helpful.

Universities and Community Colleges

Some colleges and universities, as part of their extension/outreach programs, periodically give courses and hold seminars or workshops to assist people of "retirement age" in getting a clearer idea of the kinds of activities they'd like to pursue.

For example, James K., 66, was a marketing professor for almost 40 years. He took an "Unretirement" course at the Center for Creative Retirement of the University of North Carolina at Asheville. During this course, participants closely examined their strengths, skills, and experiences and made plans for re-entering the workplace.

Yellow Pages

Looking for local companies in certain businesses? The Yellow Pages may be one of your better sources, especially for locating smaller firms.

If you're looking for a for-profit job, check for directory sections such as "Employment Concerns" and "Self-Help and Support Groups." In my area directory, for example, there's a listing titled "Forty Plus of Philadelphia (Provides Training & Resources to Find a Job for Managerial & Professionals Only)."

If it's volunteer opportunities you seek, look in your phone book for a section called "Community Action Pages" or something similar. Under a subsection, such as "Human Services," you may find an agency that deals specifically with your concerns.

If you want to find a company or organization located outside of your locality, you can get its address and telephone number from SuperPages.com's Web site at <www.superpages.com>; however, don't expect the results always to be accurate.

Sources for Determining Transferable Skills

As the name implies, transferable skills can be used in almost any occupation. Unless you're staying in the same occupation, you'll want to think of yourself—and describe yourself to others—in terms of transferable skills.

If you have trouble determining your transferable skills, here are two sources that can help:

- Richard Bolles's book, *What Color Is Your Parachute?* (Berkeley: Ten Speed Press, 2003 edition), offers a list of 246 transferable skills, along with discussion and exercises to help you identify yours.
- The Web site of Wisconsin's Department of Workforce Development, <www.dwd.state.wi.us/dwd/publications/223e_28a.htm>, has a brief discussion about transferable skills and a list of over 200 of them.

Self-Administered Career Tests

If *that* career is still illusive after you've read through Step 5 and completed the Renaissance Discovery Summary, consider taking some self-administered career tests. These take only a short amount of time (usually 10 to 40 minutes), and they may crystallize your thinking.

ONLINE TESTS. There are a host of online tests. I've spent hours examining and taking many of these tests, mostly those recommended by experts. Here's a tip that'll save you time: Take only the CISS (the Campbell Interest and Skill Survey), a test used by many career counselors. You'll find it at <www.profiler.com/ciss>. The cost is $17.95. There are 320 multiple choice (technically "semantic differential") questions, and it'll take approximately 25–40 minutes to complete the test.

There are a number of reasons I recommend this particular test:

- ➤ It relates your scores directly to careers that are most suited for you. You'll get a 15-page report suggesting which careers you should pursue, develop, explore, or avoid. It also shows how your test results compare with the scores of happily employed people in those careers.
- ➤ Interested in seeking out new hobbies? The report also gives insight into which activities you should develop or pursue.
- ➤ You can also access the CISS Career Planner, an 18-page guide that includes exercises, explanations, and illustrations that will help you translate your test results into action.

PRINTED TESTS. One book that's a must is Richard Bolles's best seller (over 7 million copies in print) *What Color Is Your Parachute?* (Berkeley: Ten Speed Press, 2003 edition). Although parts of the book may not be applicable to you, you'll find Chapters 7–9 and Appendix A most useful in determining your interests.

To take a look at other books, try an online book store such as <www.bn.com> or <www.amazon.com>. Use the search term "career tests." You'll get listings of scores of books. For those books that seem like good sources, examine the tables of contents and comments from critics and readers.

Career Counselors and Life Coaches

Perhaps you'd feel more comfortable if you had a personal consultation with a career counselor. Don't think you're going to get that great revelation, that divine moment when you say, "Ah ha! Now I finally know who I am and what I should do." But you can usually count on gaining a better grasp of your skills and interests and a firmer knowledge of likely careers, as well as some good ideas about how to position yourself and locate a job in your chosen field.

On the other hand, if what you're seeking is a better balance between your personal and professional life—and if you want to bring about action—then consider a professional/personal coach.

Finding a good career counselor or life coach is often not easy, and in most states these are unregulated fields. Your best bet is to rely on recommendations from relatives and friends. If you don't have such a personal reference for a career counselor, look for one who is a National Certified Career Counselor. For selecting a coach, see Laura Berman Fortgang, *Take Yourself to the Top*, Warner Books, 1998, pp. 211–213.

What will this cost? Usually somewhere around $100 an hour. Make sure you understand all the fees before you start your first session. Don't—repeat, *don't*—work with any career counselor who insists on a long-term contract. Work only with a career counselor who charges by the session. As for a coach's fees, because of the nature of the coaching process, an initial three-month contract is usually standard.

FREE COUNSELING RESOURCES. Some communities offer free counseling programs for residents over a certain age. In my area, for example, there's a program for people over 55. It provides career professionals to assess skills, interests, experience, and education and to assist in identifying jobs for which participants are well suited.

Many public libraries also offer career information centers for adults. Such centers provide, among other things, free assistance in exploring careers and preparing résumés as well as information about other agencies that can help with career planning and training.

Renaissance Idea Stimulators

Looking for a renaissance career? Here are almost 200 ideas. Even if one of these doesn't suit your needs, you can still benefit from scanning the lists. Highly creative people build huge mental fact files that they use to generate creative solutions. Browsing through these opportunities may spark ideas that will lead you to your career.

Interested in volunteer work? See the listings that begin below. If you're more interested in a for-profit venture, turn to page 169.

Volunteer Opportunities

In Appendix A, p. 155, I mentioned several clearing-houses for volunteers and organizations seeking volunteers.

If you want an even better notion of opportunities available, look over the following lists of possibilities. These lists are divided into two categories; opportunities primarily within the United States and those available in other countries.

In case you'd like more information about a specific organization, I've included telephone numbers and/or Web sites.

If you want a detailed lowdown on the world of volunteering, get a copy of Hope Eagan's *Volunteering: An Easy, Smart Guide to Volunteering* (Barnes & Noble Basics, 2001). It's the most up-to-date and comprehensive book of its type that I've seen.

Volunteer Opportunities
Primarily Within the United States

Abortion Issues
   Planned Parenthood Federation of America,
      <www.plannedparenthood.org>
   National Right to Life, 202-626-8800
Amnesty
   Amnesty International (USA), 212-807-8400, <www.aiusa.org>
Animal Protection/Rehabilitation
   Defenders of Wildlife, 202-289-4814
   The National Wildlife Rehabilitators Association, 612-259-4086
   National Wildlife Federation, 800-822-9919, <www.nwf.org>
   U.S. Fish and Wildlife Service, <www.volunteer.gov/gov>
Archeology
   U.S. National Park Service, <www.volunteer.gov/gov>
   University Research Expeditions Program, University of California,
      510-642-6586
Arts Education
   Young Audiences, 800-836-0494, <www.youngaudiences.org>
Assistance to Military Personnel
   Army Community Service, <www.goacs.org>
   Navy–Marine Corps Relief Society, <www.nmcrs.org>
   United Service Organizations/USO, 202-610-5700, <www.uso.org>
Back Country/Wilderness
   U.S. Government, <www.volunteer.gov/gov>
Ballroom Dancing
   U.S. Ballroom Dance Association, 800-447-9047, <www.usabda.org/
      home/index.cfm>
Birding
   American Birding Association, 800-835-2473
Botany
   American Association of Botanical Gardens and Arboreta,
      <www.aabga.org>
   U.S. Government, <www.volunteer.gov/gov>
Caregiving/People with Disabilities or Infirmities
   Easter Seals, 800-221-6827, <www.easter-seals.org>
   Hospice Foundation, 800-854-3402, <www.hospicefoundation.org>
   Independent Living Center, <www.ilusa.com>
   Lighthouse for the Blind, 800-829-0500, <www.lighthouse.org>

National Mental Health Association, <www.nmha.org>
United Way, <www.unitedway.org>
Caregiving/Economically Underprivileged
   Association of Community Organizations for Reform Now/
      ACORN, < www.acorn.org>
   Habitat for Humanity, 800-372-7986, <www.habitat.org>
   National Coalition for the Homeless, 202-737-6444,
      <www.nationalhomeless.org>
   National Interfaith Hospitality Networks, 908-272-1100,
      <www.nihn.org>
   Second Harvest (hunger relief), <www.secondharvest.org>
Campground Hosts (National Parks)
   U.S. Government Department of Agriculture, Forest Service,
      <www.volunteer.gov/gov>
Cartography
   U.S. Geological Survey, National Mapping Division, 703-648-4000
   U.S. Geological Survey, Volunteer Program Coordinator, 703-648-
      7452
Civil Air Patrol
   Civil Air Patrol, <www.capnhq.gov>
Coast Guard
   U.S. Coast Guard Auxiliary, <www.cgaus.org>
Computers
   U.S. Government, <www.volunteer.gov/gov>
Conservation (Education)
   U.S. Government, <www.volunteer.gov/gov>
Conservation (Land)
   U.S. Government, <www.volunteer.gov/gov>
Conservation (Natural Resource Planning)
   U.S. Government, <www.volunteer.gov/gov>
Conservation (Water)
   Ocean Conservancy, 202-429-5609, <www.oceanconservancy.org>
   U.S. Government, <www.volunteer.gov/gov>
Construction and Maintenance
   U.S. Government, <www.volunteer.gov/gov>
Counseling Nonprofit Organizations & Businesses
   National Executive Service Corps, management counseling to non-
      profit organizations, 212-269-1234, <www.nesc.org>
   Service Corps of Retired Executives (SCORE), management coun-
      seling to small businesses, 800-634-0245, <www.score.org>

Community Restoration
    Habitat for Humanity, 800-372-7986, <www.habitat.org>
Crime Prevention/Neighborhood Watch
    National Crime Prevention Council, 202-466-6272, <www.ncpc.org>
Disaster Relief
    American Red Cross, 877-272-7337, <www.redcross.org>
Disease Eradication/Prevention/Control
    Alzheimer's Association, 800-272-3900, <www.alz.org>
    American Cancer Society, 800-ACS-2345, <www.cancer.org>
    American Diabetes Association, 800-242-8721, <www.diabetes.org>
    American Heart Association, 800-242-8721, <www.americanheart.
        org>
    Arthritis Foundation, 800-283-7800, <www.arthritis.org>
    Muscular Dystrophy Association of America, 480-496-4530
    National Childhood Cancer Foundation, 202-234-6020
    Parkinson's Disease Foundation, 800-457-6676, <www.pdf.org>
    U.S. Government, <www.volunteer.gov/gov>
Domestic Violence
    Abuse against children: Court Appointed Special Advocate/CASA,
        800-628-3233, <www.nationalcasa.org>
    Abuse against women: National Coalition Against Domestic
        Violence, 303-839-1852, <www.ncadv.org>
Drunken Driving
    Mothers Against Drunk Driving, 800-438-6233, <www.madd.org>
Elder Care
    Little Brothers/Friends of the Elderly, 312-829-3055,
        <www.littlebrothers.org>
    Meals on Wheels Association of America, <www.projectmeal.org>
Fire-Fighter Support
    International Fire Buff Associates, <www.ifba.org>
Foster Care
    National Court Appointed Special Advocate Association (support-
        ing children in foster care), 800-628-3233
Genealogy Research
    Genealogy Today, <www.genealogytoday.com>
    Random Acts of Genealogical Kindness, <www.raogk.org>
Hiking
    The American Discovery Trail, <www.discoverytrail.org>
    American Hiking Society, 301-565-6704, <www.americanhiking.
        org>

Historical Preservation
   National Trust for Historic Preservation, 202-588-6000
   The OASIS Institute (oral history), 314-862-2933
   U.S. Government, <www.volunteer.gov/gov>
Illiteracy
   Literacy Volunteers of America, <www.literacyvolunteers.org>
   Reading is FUNdamental (for kids), 877-743-7323, <www.rif.org>
Libraries
   Friends of Libraries, USA, 312-7437-4907
   U.S. Government, <www.volunteer.gov/gov>
Mentoring/Working with Young People
   America's Promise (Colin Powell's program),
     <www.americaspromise.org>
   AmeriCorps, 202-606-5000, <www.americorps.org>
   Big Brothers/Big Sisters of America, 215-567-7000,
     <www.bbbsa.org>
   Boys & Girls Clubs of America, 404-487-5700, <www.bgca.org>
   Boy Scouts and Cub Scouts, <www.scouting.org>
   Camp Fire Boys and Girls, 816-756-7000
   Cities in Schools, 703-519-8999, <cis@cisnet.org>
   Covenant House (at-risk youths), 212-727-4000
   4-H, United States Department of Agriculture, Extension Service,
     202-720-2908
   Help One Student to Succeed, 800-833-4678, <www.hosts.com>
   National Association of Service & Conservation Corps (tutorial
     support for at-risk youths), 202-737-6272, <www.nascc.org>
   National Mentoring Partnership,703-224-2200,
     <www.mentoring.org>
Museums
   American Association for Museum Volunteers, 202-289-1818,
     <www.aam-us.org>
Political Organizations
   Democratic National Committee, 202-863-8000
   Republican National Committee, 202-863-8500
Preserving National Parks
   Department of Interior, <www.volunteer.gov/gov>
Prisoners
   Volunteer Today (the volunteer magazine of the Bureau of Prisons),
     <www.bop.gov>
Range/Livestock
   U.S. Government, <www.volunteer.gov/gov>

Refugees
>   Church World Service, 888-297-1516, <www.churchworldservice.
>   org>
>   International Rescue Committee, <www.theirc.org>
>   Orphanages.Org, <www.orphanages.org>
>   UNICEF, 800-367-5437, <www.unicefusa.org>
>   World Relief, <www.wr.org>

Science Projects
>   U.S. Government, <www.volunteer.gov/gov>

Sister Cities
>   Sister Cities International, 202-347-8630

Sports
>   U.S. Olympic Committee, <www.olympic-usa.org>. (This Web site
>   also links to various other sports organizations, such as ones for
>   the disabled.)

Symphony
>   The American Symphony Orchestra League, 202-776-0212

Timber/Fire Prevention
>   U.S. Government, <www.volunteer.gov/gov>

Trail/Campground Maintenance
>   U.S. Government, <www.volunteer.gov/gov>

Tour Guide/Interpretation
>   U.S. Government, <www.volunteer.gov/gov>

TV Monitoring
>   Parents Television Council, <www.parentstv.org>

Travelers Assistance
>   National Council for International Visitors, 800-523-8101,
>   <www.nciv.org>
>   Travelers Aid International, 202-546-1127

Weather Watcher
>   The National Weather Service, 301-713-0622, <www.weather.gov>

Weed/Invasive Species Control
>   U.S. Government, <www.volunteer.gov/gov>

Overseas Volunteer Opportunities

Perhaps a volunteer career overseas may provide the "why"
you've been looking for. Different cultures, customs, geogra-
phy, climates—whatever—may give you a zest for living.

Don't expect a vacation. Count on a challenge. Living conditions may be primitive. The work you do may be menial. Still, you may find it rewarding.

It probably won't be a freebee. Many, perhaps most, organizations expect you to pay for your own transportation, and they may also stipulate that you cover your living expenses.

In some instances, knowledge of the local language is not necessary. Nor is pre-departure training. In other cases, such as a volunteer assignment with the Peace Corps, some fluency with the language and extensive training may be necessary before your leave.

If you're reluctant to make a long-term commitment—say, a year or two—you can still make a career out of piecing together a number of short-term commitments.

The following lists of organizations fall into two categories: those who are seek volunteers for short-term assignments and those who want volunteers to commit for a year or more.

Short Term Assignments
(usually less than a month)

Amigos de las Americas, 800-231-7796, <www.amigoslink.org>
Amizade (renovating schools), 888-973-4443, <www.amizade.org>
B'nai B'rith Israel Commission, 202-857-6646, <www.bnaibrith.org>
Citizens' Development Corps (technical assistance and training for
     small businesses), 202-530-7660, <www.cdc.org>
Cross Cultural Solutions (teaching), 800-380-4777, <www.
     crossculturalsolutions.org>
Earthwatch (conservation projects), 800-776-0188,
     <www.earthwatch.org>
Financial Services Volunteer Corps (financial advice to governmental
     agencies), <www.fsvc.org>
Food for the Hungry International, 800-248-6437, <www.fh.org>
Global Volunteers, 800-487-1074, <www.globalvolunteers.org>
Habitat for Humanity, <www.habitat.org>
Heifer Project International, 800-422-1311, <www.heifer.org>
MADRE, INC. (women's rights), 212-627-0444, <www.madre.org>
Ocean Society Expeditions (biodiversity), 800-326-7421

University Research Expeditions Program (assisting with research),
    510-642-6586
Volunteers for Peace (teaching), 802-259-2759. <www.vfp.org>
World Concern, 206-546-7201, <www.worldconcern.org>

Longer-Term Assignments

CONCERN/America, 714-953-8575, <www.concernamerica.org>
Cross Cultural Solutions (teaching), 800-380-4777,
        <www.crossculturalsolutions.org>
Peace Corps, 800-424-8580, <www.peacecorps.org>
WorldTeach, 617-495-5527, <www.worldteach.org>

Opportunities for Healthcare Specialists
(both short- and long-term)

Doctors of the World, 888-817-4357, <www.doctorsoftheworld.org>
Doctors Without Borders, <www.doctorswithoutborders.org>
Health Volunteers Overseas, <www.hvousa.org>
International Medical Volunteers Association, <www.imva.org>
Project Concern International, 858-279-9690,
        <www.projectconcerninternational.org>
Volunteer Optometric Service to Humanity, <www.vosh.org>

For-Profit Ventures

Perhaps you're seeking a renaissance career where you can be
your own boss and/or work from home. Here are many possibilities. Should you want more information about certain careers, there is always the Internet. And for many of the career
opportunities, I've recommended comprehensive, up-to-date,
easy-to-get books.

Accounting Services: See Jack Fox, *Starting and Building Your Own Ac-
    counting Business,* John Wiley & Sons, 1999.
Bed-and-Breakfast Owner/Operator: See Park Davis and Susannah
    Craig, *Complete Idiot's Guide to Running a Bed and Breakfast,* Pen-
    guin Group, 2001.
Building and Marketing Furniture: See Blair Howard, *Making Money
    Making Furniture,* F & W Publications, 1999.

Buying and Selling Businesses: See Garrett Sutton, *How to Buy and Sell a Business*, Warner Books, 2003.

Buying and Selling Real Estate: See Robert Irwin and Richard Jorgensen, *Buy, Rent and Sell: How to Profit by Investing in Residential Real Estate*, McGraw-Hill, 2001.

Catering: See Denise Vivaldo, *How to Start a Home-Based Catering Business*, 4th edition, Globe Pequot, 2002.

Coin Operated Laundry Owner/Manager: See Mandy Erickson, *Start Your Own Coin-Operated Laundry*, Entrepreneur Press, 2003.

Consultant. See Alan Weiss, *Getting Started in Consulting*, John Wiley & Sons, 2000.

Craft and Hobby Business (for example, ceramics, decorative painting, glassmaking, kite making, leather working, metal working, and woodworking and carving): See William G. Hynes, *Start and Run a Craft Business*, 7th edition, Self-Counsel Press, 2002, and Barbara Arena, *The Complete Idiot's Guide to Making Money with Your Hobby*, Alpha Books, 2001.

Cruise Ship Lecturer

Deck and Patio Designer: See Paula Marshall (ed.), *Deck and Patio Planner*, Better Homes and Gardens, 2001.

Delivering Cars

Desktop Publisher

Elder Services (for example, relocating, limousine, and home care)

Event Planner: See Judy Allen, *Event Planning: The Ultimate Guide to Successful Meetings, Corporate Events, Fundraising, Galas . . .* , John Wiley & Sons, 2000.

Fiction and/or Nonfiction Writer

Financial Advisor: See Jeffery H. Rattiner, *Getting Started as a Financial Planner*, Bloomberg Press, 2000.

Franchising a Business: See Erwin J. Keup, *Franchise Bible: How to Buy a Franchise or Franchise Your Own Business*, 4th edition, Oasis Press/PSI Research, 2000.

Freelance Photographer: See Cliff Hollenbeck and Nancy Hollenbeck, *Freelance Photographer's Handbook*, Amherst Media, 1999.

Genealogical research

Grant Writer: See Beverly A. Browning, *How to Become a Grant Writing Consultant*, Beverly Browning & Associates, 2000, and *Grant Writing for Dummies*, John Wiley & Sons, 2001.

Herb Gardener: See Mimi Luebbermann, *Sell What You Grow: How to Take Your Herbs and Produce to Market for Serious Cash*, Crown, 2000.

Home Inspector: See Claire Ginther, *How to Start a Home Inspection Business: Your Step-By-Step Guide to Success*, Entrepreneur Media, 2003.

Hydoponic Farmer

Import/Export Business: See Rob Adams and Terry Adams, *How to Start an Export/Import Business*, Entrepreneur Press, 2003.

Internet Business: See Susan Sweeney, *101 Internet Businesses You Can Start From Home*, Maximum Press, 2001.

Inventing Toys and Games: See Richard C. Levy and Ronald O. Weingartner, *The Toy and Game Inventor's Handbook*, Alpha, 2003.

Landscape Architect: See Owen E. Dell, *How to Start a Landscaping Business*, Globe Pequot Press, 2003.

Life Coach: See Michelle J. McGarvey, *Train at Home to Become a Certified Personal/Life Coach*, Writers Club Press, 2003.

Mail-Order Business (for example, boating supplies, computer software, garden seeds, gift baskets, gourmet foods, hunting supplies, nuts, popcorn, and pilot supplies): See Tyler G. Hicks, *101 Great Mail-Order Businesses*, revised 2nd edition, Prima Publishing, 2000.

Manufacturer's Representative

Market Researcher

Newsletter or Magazine Publisher (for example, industry trends and investment advice): See Cheryl Woodward, *Starting & Running a Successful Newsletter or Magazine*, 3rd edition, Nolo Press, 2002.

Organic Farmer: See Roger Yepsen (ed.), *1,001 Old-Time Garden Tips: Timeless Bits of Wisdom on How to Grow Everything Organically, From the Good Old Days When Everyone Did*, Rodale Press, 1998.

Pet Care: See Kathy R. Salzberg, *How to Start a Home-Based Pet Care Business*, Globe Pequot Press, 2002.

Professional Actor: See Brian O'Neil, *Acting as a Business: Strategies for Success*, 2nd edition, Reed Elsevier, 1999.

Raising Animals (for example, commercial animals such as cattle and sheep, exotic animals like ostriches or llamas, or domestic animals like pets)

Real Estate Agent: See Darryl Davis, *How to Become a Power Agent in Real Estate*, McGraw-Hill, 2002.

Relocation Specialist

Remodeling Contractor

Restaurateur: See Elizabeth Lawrence, *The Complete Restaurateur*, updated edition, Penguin Group, 2001.

Restoration Services

Security Specialist
Shopping Services
Stock Broker
Tax Consultant: See Gary W. Carter, *Getting Started in Tax Consulting*, John Wiley & Sons, 2001.
Technical Writer: See Janet VanWicklin, *The Tech Writer's Survival Guide: A Comprehensive Handbook for Aspiring Technical Writers*, revised edition, Facts on File, 2001.
Travel Writer: See Cynthia Dial, *Teach Yourself Travel Writing*, McGraw-Hill, 2001.

APPENDIX C

Planning Manual

In this appendix, you'll find all the forms (and instructions) for planning your renaissance. If you'd like more information on completing your plan, take a look at the case example.

Charting Your Course (The Master Plan)

DESCRIPTIVE PLANS. For some categories, all that's needed is to note the amount of time you'd like to spend on them. For others, you should also describe the activity (action plan). Page 195 offers examples.

SEQUENCED PLANS. You may have some categories involving a number of activities that need to be carried out. Most likely, you will have some that need to be done in sequence and others that can be done at the same time. In these instances, follow five guidelines (p. 196 offers an example):

1. List activities that need to be accomplished according to *when* they need to be accomplished.
2. Estimate the amount of time each activity will require.
3. Set a completion date for each activity.
4. Expect backtracking and adjustments. As you go through the process, you'll probably think of additional activities,

some of which need to be done early in the sequence. Also, once you start totaling time requirements, you may have to revise your starting date, your completion date, or your plan.

5. Don't strive for perfection. Being directionally correct is better than having "analysis paralysis." Besides, once you put your plan into action, you'll always discover changes you have to make.

"THINGS TO DO" LISTS. If you're continually short of ideas for activities for some categories, consider scouting around and putting together lists of things to do at a later date. These lists can be attached to your Master Plan. (Page 196 gives an example.)

You'll find two blank Master Plan Worksheets on the following pages.

Scheduling Your Activities

You should be able to complete a Weekly Scheduling Worksheet in 15 minutes or so. You may want to use your present appointment calendar. On the other hand, if your calendar has limited space for recording planned activities, you may want to use the forms on pp. 180–183 (enlarged if you choose) and reserve your calendar for appointments.

Here are six guidelines (pp. 200–201 provide an example):

1. *Make time to plan.* Although it will take only 10 to 15 minutes to schedule your week's activities, you'll never *find* time to do it. You'll have to *make* time. Why not set aside a specific time on Friday or Saturday of the week before, or perhaps on Sunday?

2. *Schedule the forthcoming week.* Focus on that week. Of course, as you've always done, you'll schedule some activities

Master Plan Worksheet

Activity	Time Allocation	Action Plan	Completion Date

Master Plan Worksheet

Activity	Time Allocation	Action Plan	Completion Date

Master Plan Worksheet

weeks in advance—football games, workshops and seminars, vacations.

Take a look at your appointment calendar. Probably some of the time slots will already be accounted for: a doctor's appointment Monday morning at 10:00; dinner with friends Friday night. If you have days that are completely clear, mentally bookmark them.

Examine your time allotments for your various categories, such as career, time with family, and exercise. Then see if there are any activities on your Master Plan that should be on the docket for this week.

Which activities require large blocks of time? Once you've put these on your calendar, fill in around them.

As a practical matter, you're not even going to come close to filling in all the time slots when you put together your weekly schedule. Maybe you'll account for only one-third of your discretionary time, or less, because of contingencies.

For example, you want to have a meeting with a particular person sometime during the week. But the day and time are up to him, and he said he'd couldn't let you know until Tuesday. So you'll have to keep some times open later in the week.

And you want to have some flexibility. For example, you run into a friend at the post office and it's a must to have lunch with him that week.

But schedule as many hours as you can. It's good to start the week off running, with many activities scheduled and well in mind.

3. *Schedule throughout the week.* Try to follow this rule: have the forthcoming day scheduled in detail.

Check your calendar every evening or the first thing in the morning. You'll typically have open times for that day or for later days in the week. Some of these openings will occur because the time periods were never scheduled, others because of changes in your plans or cancellations.

Decide on ways to put these open periods to good use. Take a moment to think about how you're coming along with your overall time allocations. What categories are you neglecting? What activities could be plugged into the open time slots?

Keep your calendar at hand throughout the day. As you know, cancellations and changes are the rule, not the exception.

4. *Examine your schedule with an eye toward efficient use of time.* For example:

> ➤ Can you set aside one afternoon for errands, paying bills, doctor appointments, picking up your dry cleaning, and so forth, so that you'll have uninterrupted blocks of time for other categories, such as your career?
> ➤ Can you combine activities? Can you do a disagreeable activity (the treadmill) while you are doing a more agreeable one (watching *Inside Politics*)?

5. *Plan to do something special every day.* Regardless of your age or health, today is the only day you can count on. Make the most of it.

The "something special" doesn't have to take up the entire day. It may just be a short walk with your significant other. Time on the practice tee. A visit to a specialty wine shop. Lunch with a person who always cheers you up.

6. *Don't let time allocations be straitjackets.* On some days, too, you'll just want to bag your routine. You may want to take a drive in the country on one of those delightful, hoar-frosted mornings when the leaves are turning. Or you may want to do what Rick, the maker of high-end bamboo fly rods, sometimes does: have breakfast, throw a log on the fire, and read a good book.

Take that drive. Read that book. Do what you want to when you want to. Live life to the fullest.

Scheduling discretionary time should not become a box that you can't get out of. It's simply a way to help you, over the long haul, spend time the way you'd really like to.

You'll find two blank Weekly Scheduling Worksheets on the following pages.

Monitoring Your Course

Time Analysis Worksheet

The Time Analysis Worksheet will help you analyze how you actually spend your time in relation to your planned schedule. Using the worksheet is simple.

A warning. I said the process is *simple,* and that's right. But it's not easy. It requires discipline to record your activities, day after day.

However, the payoffs are there. Try using the Time Analysis Worksheet for several weeks. The results will surprise you.

Following are four guidelines for using the Time Analysis Worksheet:

1. Keep track, on a day-to-day basis, of how you actually spend your time. Look at your Weekly Scheduling Worksheet. What did you have planned? What did you actually do? When there's a difference, cross out your planned activities and write in what actually happened. If you had unscheduled time periods, write in what you did during those times.
2. Make these recordings every day—religiously. Put them off for a day or two and you'll have a hard time recalling how you spent your time. Why not record your actual times when you're checking your next day's activities?

Weekly Scheduling Worksheet (Week of __________)

Time	Sunday	Monday	Tuesday
6–7 A.M.			
7–8			
8–9			
9–10			
10–11			
11–12			
12–1 P.M.			
1–2			
2–3			
3–4			
4–5			
5–6			
6–7			
7–8			
8–9			
9–10			
10–11			
11–12			

Weekly Scheduling Worksheet *(continued)*

Wednesday	Thursday	Friday	Saturday

Weekly Scheduling Worksheet (Week of __________)

Time	Sunday	Monday	Tuesday
6–7 A.M.			
7–8			
8–9			
9–10			
10–11			
11–12			
12–1 P.M.			
1–2			
2–3			
3–4			
4–5			
5–6			
6–7			
7–8			
8–9			
9–10			
10–11			
11–12			

Weekly Scheduling Worksheet *(continued)*

Wednesday	Thursday	Friday	Saturday

3. At the end of the week, total the time spent on each activity. Record these totals on the Time Analysis Worksheet.
4. Match actual times against planned time allocations. Did you spend too much time on certain activities? Neglect others? Variations should even out over a four-week period. If there's a wide divergence between time allocated and time spent, think about new allocations or new plans.

You'll find two blank Time Analysis Worksheets on the following pages.

A Case Example

Perhaps you'd like further guidance for analyzing your Renaissance Discovery Summary, developing a Master Plan, or using Weekly Scheduling Worksheets. Then read the following story of how one person started his journey toward renaissance by using these handy organizing formats.

Analyzing a Renaissance Discovery Summary

A person I'll call Pete D. has a small, but very profitable, retail store. The main products are trophies, plaques, and custom engraving. The shop is located in a medium-size northeastern city that is also the home of a major university. Most of Pete's customers are affiliated, in some way, with the university community.

Pete has been in business for more than 30 years. Previously he was a high school chemistry teacher.

When Pete first opened his shop, it was a one-person business. Over the years it has grown, and Pete now has 14 employees and a manager. The manager has been with Pete for seven years. Pete has a great deal of confidence in him, so usually Pete comes and goes as he pleases. Pete also feels that he

Time Analysis Worksheet

Activity	Time Allo-cated	Time Spent				Total
		Week 1	Week 2	Week 3	Week 4	
Career						
Family						
Religion						
Volunteer work						
Existing friends						
New friends						
Clubs, associations						
Investments						
Physical fitness						
Self-improvement						
Errands, doctor visits, etc.						
Avocations, hobbies						
Other						
Total						

Time Analysis Worksheet

Activity	Time Allo-cated	Time Spent				
		Week 1	Week 2	Week 3	Week 4	Total
Career						
Family						
Religion						
Volunteer work						
Existing friends						
New friends						
Clubs, associations						
Investments						
Physical fitness						
Self-improvement						
Errands, doctor visits, etc.						
Avocations, hobbies						
Other						
Total						

can get away from his shop for frequent two-to-three-week vacations.

He has only one other business enterprise, a rental property. Pete has good mechanical skills and enjoys making minor improvements at his store, his house, and the rental property. He uses craftsmen for major jobs, but he (like all of us) often gets irritated trying to find workmen to do projects when he wants them done and the way he wants them done.

Pete is 73. When he took his annual physical last spring, his doctor pronounced him in excellent health.

Pete has been married for almost 50 years. He and Betty met at the local university, and they have lived in this city ever since then. Betty is also in excellent health.

They have four grown children in their late 30s or early 40s and two grandchildren in their teens. Two of their children live within 20 minutes of them; the other two are less than a two-hour drive away.

Pete's hobbies are reading, traveling, eating out, going to the theater, and, to a lesser extent, fishing.

In many ways Pete's life seems ideal. He and his wife have a good relationship and are on excellent terms with their children. Pete has enough money to live comfortably, and his business allows him a great deal of freedom.

Yet he's restless. At times, depressed.

Pete is tired of his business. A skilled engraver, he used to find that work challenging. Now it's tedious and boring. Most of the problems he encounters are the same ones he's been dealing with for years: hiring new employees, firing those who don't fit in; coping with idiotic government regulations.

As he looks ahead, he knows that he'll have more challenges, some new and some the same. He knows he could handle them. Yet he lacks the enthusiasm and energy to do so, simply because he'd rather be doing something else.

But what?

I asked Pete to fill out the various Renaissance Discovery worksheets and the Renaissance Discovery Summary. Take a look at Pete's completed summary worksheet (p. 189) and his written analysis of his search descriptors (below).

Pete's Written Analysis of His Key Search Descriptors

I'm most interested in engaging in some type of for-profit business, preferably building and construction, where I can be creative, set goals (achievement oriented), initiate (be assertive), live in the Southwest in a safe environment, and be able to travel and have adventure.

Let's see what insights Pete could derive from his key search descriptors. By ranking, quantitatively, the criteria most important to him, Pete has developed a clearer picture of the object of his search. These criteria will help keep Pete from wandering down paths that—for him—would lead to nowhere. For one thing, some of the career paths discussed in Step 4 can be dismissed out of hand.

- ▸ Continuing to Work for Your Present Employer: Obviously not relevant.
- ▸ Starting to Work for a New Employer: This career path, too, can be dismissed quickly. Considering Pete's desire for flexible hours (especially taken in context with the work schedule he's accustomed to), his business background, his age, and his high-ranking personal trait of assertiveness, working for someone else might be, for him, more like the dark ages than a renaissance.
- ▸ Continuing Your Business: It might be different if Pete didn't like his business because of rigid hours or a lack of

Pete's Renaissance Discovery Summary Worksheet

Time Allocations
(in hours, 10 items max.)

Career	20
Family	6
Religion	
Volunteer work	
Existing friends	5
New friends	
Clubs, associations	
Investments	20
Physical fitness	5
Self-improvement	13
Errands, doctor visits, etc.	5

Avocations, hobbies *(specify):*

Home/garden	8

Other *(specify):*

TOTAL   82

Preferences

Payoffs (in rank order, with scores)

1.	Monetary	5
2.	Adventure/travel	4
3.	Stimulate creativity	4
4.	Intellectual stimulation	2
5.	Promote a cause	1

Personal Traits (in rank order, with scores)

1.	Achievement oriented	5
2.	Assertive	5
3.	Objective	4
4.	Generous	3
5.	Adventuresome/pioneering	3

Environment (in rank order, with scores)

1.	Live in the Southwest	7
2.	Safe environment	6
3.	New, different types of work	5
4.	Building, creating	5
5.	Flexible work schedule	4

Use of Skills (in rank order, with scores and skill proficiencies)

1.	Leading/initiating	6	6
2.	Building/constructing	5	9
3.	Conceptualizing/designing programs	4	7
4.	Analyzing data	3	5
5.	Growing plants	2	8

free time—he might be able to work that out. But he's looking for a new, different type of work. Furthermore, he wants to live in the Southwest. These two factors, by themselves, plainly eliminate staying with his present business.

➤ Volunteering Your Services: Can be eliminated since Pete's highest-ranking career priority was monetary.

The two remaining career paths seem promising:

➤ Pursuing an Artistic Career (Self-Employed): This path might be a possibility because Pete's a skilled engraver. Although he now finds engraving "tedious and boring," would he feel differently about engraving artistic lithography plates, for example?

➤ Starting a New Business: Opening a new business could also be compatible with Pete's time allocations, career payoffs, desired personal traits, work environment, and use of skills. And a new business might well allow Pete to move to the Southwest. I asked how Betty felt about moving to that area. She said, "Well, if things were right . . ." It seemed that their location would be primarily determined by Pete's career choice. A safe environment would also be a major criterion.

Let's take a look at three of the many kinds of businesses Pete might consider:

➤ He could open a shop similar to the one he has in the Northeast. Even though he's tired of his present business, a start-up in a new location might give him the adventure and new experiences he's seeking.

➤ Pete might follow in the footsteps of Gib, the manufacturer's representative who calls on power plants. Pete could become a manufacturer's representative for a trophy company while touring the Southwest with Betty in a luxurious RV.

> ➤ Given his interest and skills in building and construction, Pete might renovate homes for resale.

(Before continuing with this case example, you should have read Step 4 and Step 5.)

Developing a Master Plan

In Pete's Renaissance Discovery Summary Worksheet, he listed these categories and time allocations: career, 20 hours; family, 6 hours; existing friends, 5 hours; investments, 20 hours; physical fitness, 5 hours; self-improvement, 13 hours; errands, doctor visits, etc., 5 hours; and home/garden, 8 hours.

Let's see how Pete might put together his Master Plan.

Career (20 hours)

A review of Pete's Renaissance Discovery Summary reveals that he really would like to change locations, and most likely, his career. Pete's interested in running a for-profit business, preferably building and construction, where he can be creative, set goals (be achievement oriented), initiate (be assertive), be able to travel and have adventure, and live in a safe environment somewhere in the Southwest.

Let's assume that Pete decides to take a month-long exploratory trip to check out the possibility of living in the Southwest and starting a new business—renovating homes for resale.

It's now January. Pete talks with his wife and his store manager and decides that the best time for the trip would be sometime around April.

In order to make the trip productive, Pete has some planning to do. And since this prep work is new to Pete, it will pay him to develop a sequenced plan, to think through—and write out—what he should do and in what sequence, along with the time requirements and the necessary completion dates.

First, let's look at some of the things that need to be done. Pete and Betty should establish criteria for their ideal city, such as crime rate, size, growth potential, climate, community services, cultural opportunities, proximity to major medical facilities.

Next, they need to find cities that meet these yardsticks.

Once Pete has formalized his thinking about the type of re-hab homes he's interested in (neighborhood, condition of the homes, and price), he should contact realtors in the targeted cities to get some idea of the availability of appropriate properties.

Then he needs to route his trip.

He and Betty could also make this exploratory trip a mini-vacation. Why not take scenic routes whenever possible? And how about making reservations at interesting inns, bed and breakfasts, hotels, resorts?

Since prices of airline tickets vary with the destination, Pete will want to check flight prices before routing his trip. Tickets will have to be purchased at least several weeks—possibly a month—in advance. Since this will be tourist season, he may as well make reservations for a car rental at the same time.

Although Pete has had some experience in renovating homes, he may want to read a few how-to books before he and Betty leave, or perhaps even take a mini-course or two, such as those at Home Depot.

Once he's decided what needs to be done, he needs to sequence these activities, then estimate time requirements and completion dates for each activity.

While Pete is preparing for his trip, he also has his shop to manage. Although Pete's manager does a good job running the store, Pete normally checks such vital signs as key customer accounts, total sales, and cash flow, and when necessary, suggests action.

Before the trip, Pete believes he should spend at least 10 hours a week at the store looking after these aspects of the business. Since these activities are routine, a one-line descriptive plan, such as "Manage store" and a notation of the time (10 hours), will be sufficient.

Keeping to his schedule of 20 hours for his career, that would leave Pete 10 hours a week to prepare for his trip.

Of course, Pete also has to take care of all the mundane chores involved in being away for a while (stopping the papers, rerouting mail, having somebody check his house now and then), but it's hardly necessary to include these in the Master Plan. Nor would it be useful to mention that while Pete is in the Southwest, he and his manager plan to keep in touch by cell phone and fax. This is their standard practice when Pete is out of town.

Other Categories

Let's take a look at Pete's plans for his other categories: family; existing friends; investments; physical fitness; self-improvement; errands, doctor visits, etc.; and home/garden.

FAMILY (6 HOURS). Pete wants some special time with Betty—something more than day-to-day breakfasts and dinners and watching TV. The 6 hours he has allocated are for a special dinner, a play, or something else out of the ordinary.

Of course, he'd like to spend time with his grown children and grandchildren, but he thinks that special occasions—maybe once or twice a month—will be enough. After all, they have their own lives to live.

So, on a week-to-week basis, spending time with Betty is what really matters. Since Pete and Betty are not lacking ideas for what to do, as far as Pete's planning is concerned, noting the time allocation is enough.

EXISTING FRIENDS (5 HOURS). Pete and Betty have friends they like to spend time with, but usually it's just going out to dinner. These times are most always fun, but Pete—and Betty too—would like some new and different things to do. Pete decides to check the Internet for local activities that they and their friends might enjoy. Since it'll just take a few minutes of surfing, he decides to start the list of "Things to Do with Friends" as soon as he finishes his Master Plan.

INVESTMENTS (20 HOURS). Pete has a routine, reading *Forbes* and *The Wall Street Journal* and watching a number of TV programs, such as CNBC's *Power Lunch* and *Closing Bell*, as well as CNN's *Lou Dobbs Moneyline*. Pete's happy with the way he spends this time, so a one-liner noting the time allocation is probably enough.

PHYSICAL FITNESS (5 HOURS). Pete visits a health club three times a week, and he sees no reason to change. Again, a one-liner noting the time allocation is sufficient.

SELF-IMPROVEMENT (13 HOURS). Once again, this category is not a problem area. At the beginning of the week, Pete examines the TV guide to see if there are any documentaries or biographies he'd like to watch. And he's an avid reader. No need to write out an extensive plan for this category.

ERRANDS, DOCTOR VISITS, ETC. (5 HOURS). A one-liner will do just fine.

HOME/GARDEN (8 HOURS). In the summer Pete spends most of this time in the garden; in the winter, he refurbishes antiques. Again, all that's needed is a one-liner.

The next page shows Pete's Master Plan, and the page after that shows the attachments that he creates to clarify for himself two categories—career and time with friends.

(Before continuing with this case example, you should have read the section "Scheduling Your Activities" in Step 5.)

Pete's Master Plan Worksheet

Activity	Time Allocation	Action Plan	Completion Date
Career	20 hours	Manage store (10 hours) and plan for new career (10 hours—see attachment)	
Family	6 hours	Special events	ongoing
Existing friends	5 hours		ongoing
Investments	20 hours	Read publications, watch certain TV shows	ongoing
Physical fitness	5 hours	Visit health club 3 times a week	ongoing
Self-improvement	13 hours	Read, watch selected TV shows	ongoing
Errands, doctor visits, etc.	5 hours		ongoing
Home/garden	8 hours		ongoing

Pete's Attachments to His Master Plan Worksheet

Career: Action Plans, Time Requirements, and Completion Dates

1. Set up criteria for ideal cities, such as size, growth potential, climate, community services, cultural opportunities, proximity to a major medical facility. Will have to do research to help determine criteria. Time: 15 hours. Completion date: 1/25.

2. Research to find cities that meet criteria. Check, among other sources, atlases, the Internet, chambers of commerce, newspapers. Time: 15 hours. Completion date: 2/8.

3. Purchase airline tickets. Rent car. Route trip; try to follow scenic highways as much as possible. Time: 5 to 10 hours. Completion date: 2/15.

4. Research to determine criteria for rehab properties, such as neighborhood, price, condition. Time: 10 hours. Completion date: 2/15.

5. Talk with realtors in targeted cities to get general idea of availability and prices of property. Get listings. Schedule appointments? Time: 10 hours. Completion date: 2/22.

6. Find interesting places to stay on (or near) route. Make reservations. Time: 5 to 10 hours. Completion date: 3/1.

7. Schedule (weekly) any extra allocated career time to better understand buying, rehabbing, and selling properties; plan for reading on this subject, taking mini-courses, etc.

8. Target date for departure: 3/22.

Things to Do with Friends

Attend readings at bookstores
Do volunteer work for a nonprofit, such as Habitat for Humanity
Attend seminars or workshops on wine tasting, cooking, or writing
Join a good books club
Enroll in an adult evening class (such as great movies, cooking, or wine tasting)
Organize a progressive dinner or cooking club
Start a wine tasting club
Start a duplicate bridge group

Using Weekly Scheduling Worksheets

Now that we've seen Pete's Master Plan, let's look at how he might schedule his upcoming week.

It's Sunday morning. Before reading *The New York Times*, Pete decides to make out his schedule for the week.

Looking at his appointment calendar, he sees that he doesn't have to think about what to do on Friday and Saturday. He and Betty, along with another couple, are going to Boston then. Cross off those days. Except for a luncheon meeting (Monday, 11:30–1:30) with a manufacturer's rep who is pitching a new line of accessories for the store, the rest of Pete's week is clear.

Well, not quite. Normally Pete goes to a physical fitness club on Monday, Wednesday, and Friday afternoons, spending a total of about 5 hours there. This week, since he will be away on Friday, he would like to spend a few extra minutes on Monday and Wednesday on a stationary bike. Pete schedules in 3:00 to 5:00, Monday and Wednesday, for his exercise.

He glances at his overall time allotments for the remaining categories: 6 hours for family; 5 hours for existing friends; 20 hours each for career and investments; 13 hours for self-improvement; 8 hours for home/garden; and 5 hours each for physical fitness and errands.

The Boston trip will take care of time with friends and family plus hours to spare. And during the trip, Pete thinks, he'll have time to talk with Betty and their friends about some of the ideas on his "Things to Do with Friends" list.

As for his work at the store, besides meeting with the manufacturer's rep, there are some other things he needs to do, like checking inventory and calling a few suppliers. Since he can do these things at any time during the week, there is no need to schedule them now.

The trip to the Southwest, however—he'd like to get started on that right away. The first item on the agenda is coming up with criteria for ideal cities, such as city size, population growth, and availability of cultural and medical facilities. Some of the criteria seem almost obvious, but since relocating is something new for Pete, he wants to see what he can learn from others.

He decides to spend time on Monday coming up with yardsticks. First he'll check the Internet, and then he'll stop at Barnes and Noble and browse through some books. He blocks out 2:00 to 3:00 Monday afternoon and 7:00 to 10:00 Monday evening for these purposes. He also schedules in 2:00 to 5:00 on Tuesday afternoon.

He decides to wait before scheduling more time for deciding on criteria. Perhaps he can get everything done on Tuesday. Besides, he will be talking about these yardsticks with Betty throughout the week, and he can also bounce ideas off his friends during the Boston trip.

As for the time for investments, Pete has a ritual of reading *Forbes, the Wall Street Journal,* and other business publications between 8:30 and 11 in the morning. So he blocks out those times, Monday through Thursday. Since he isn't leaving for Boston until 10:00 on Friday, he also blocks out 8:00 to 9:00 that morning for reading *The Wall Street Journal.*

Thursday afternoon, he thinks, will be a good time to do errands, especially last-minute tasks before the Boston weekend. So Pete schedules 2:00 to 5:00 on Thursday for that purpose.

To schedule the self-improvement category, he checks the TV guide for educational programs. He sees that Tuesday night has a biography he wants to watch, and on Wednesday PBS is running a documentary on Frank Lloyd Wright. He schedules in those times. Pete is also reading McCullough's *Truman,* and he knows that he'll make time for that book—he can hardly put it down. Today, as soon as he finishes *The New York Times*, he's picking up *Truman*. That will take care of Sunday.

As for home/gardening, he can forget about gardening this time of the year. But he is restoring an antique chest, and he knows he'll spend some evenings on that. But for now, Pete decides, programming more of his week will be just a waste of time. He will do the rest as the week progresses. At the moment, his worksheet looks like the one on the next two pages.

Let's compare Pete's planned time allocations for a typical week with what he's scheduled for the forthcoming week:

	Master Plan	*This Week*
Career	20	
Shop		2
Southwest		7
Family	6 ⎫	
Existing friends	5 ⎭	26
Investments	20	11
Physical fitness	5	4
Self-improvement	13	11
Errands, doctor visits, etc.	5	3
Home/garden	8	0

Pete's major shortfalls are in career, investments, and home/garden. He still has a lot of open time slots that he might use for those activities, but if Pete filled those slots in now, he'd probably be overscheduling. Here's why:

First, let's look at career, where Pete has scheduled only 9 of the 20 hours. Pete is uncertain how long it will take him to nail down his parameters for ideal cities, and by Monday night he should have a better idea. Nor does he know how long it will take him to complete his projects at the store. Then, too, who knows what emergencies might arise? For now, his scheduled time for the career category is probably about right.

Pete's Weekly Scheduling Worksheet (Week of <u>January 15, 200x</u>)

Time	Sunday	Monday	Tuesday
6–7 A.M.			
7–8			
8–9		– – – – – – – investments	– – – – – – – investments
9–10		investments	investments
10–11	self-improvement	investments	investments
11–12	self-improvement	– – – – – – – shop	– – – – – – –
12–1 P.M.		shop	
1–2	self-improvement	shop – – – – – – –	
2–3	self-improvement	criteria	criteria
3–4	self-improvement	exercise	criteria
4–5	self-improvement	exercise	criteria
5–6			
6–7			
7–8		criteria	
8–9	self-improvement	criteria	self-improvement
9–10	self-improvement	criteria	
10–11			
11–12			

Pete's Weekly Scheduling Worksheet *(continued)*

Wednesday	Thursday	Friday	Saturday
– – – – – – –	– – – – – – –	investments	
investments	investments		
investments	investments	Boston	Boston
investments	investments	Boston	Boston
		Boston (criteria)	Boston
		Boston (criteria)	Boston
		Boston (list)	Boston
	errands	Boston (list)	Boston
exercise	errands	Boston	Boston
exercise	errands	Boston	Boston
		Boston	Boston
		Boston	Boston
		Boston	Boston
		Boston	Boston
self-improvement		Boston	Boston
self-improvement			

Now consider investments. Pete will spend time watching CNBC's *Power Lunch* and *Closing Bell,* as well as CNN's *Lou Dobbs Moneyline.* Count on that. Once he adds in time for those programs, he'll be closer to his 20 hours.

As for home/garden, it's hard to keep Pete from working on the antique chest he's refurbishing. Yes, Pete will make time for that activity.

Overall, Pete's weekly schedule, as of Sunday morning, is reasonably well laid out. He will fill in more of the time slots later in the week.

Of course, at the end of each day—or the beginning of the next—Pete should make sure that the upcoming day is scheduled. While scheduling activities, he should keep in mind his time allocations.

Notes

Interviews

Of the hundreds of people interviewed, only a few are referenced in this book. Some of the people depicted here refer to themselves as "retired" when actually they are pursing occupations or professions that they consider to be their life's work. Their occupations meet the dictionary definition of a career, so I describe them in that fashion.

These interviews were conducted between May 2000 and October 2002. In many instances, individuals were interviewed more than once. In such cases, they are listed below by the year of their first interview.

2000. Abby Z., Bill M., Don C., E.J., Fred M., John H., Lloyd D., Margaret S., Dr. Norm G., Pat S., Tony T., and Vernon P.

2001. Al O., Bob B., Doug W., Helen O., Irv T., Joe S., John S., Ken H., Larry K., Len W., Mary N., Mel H., Dr. Oliver G., Ray E., Dr. Richard N., Ted F., Tom M., Tom W., and Warren O.

2002. Bob B., Hugh M., Lou P., Rick R., and Dr. Walter W.

Published References

Introduction

p. 2, survey conducted by Roper Starch: Reported by Paula Mergenhagen, "Rethinking Retirement, *American Demographics*, June, 1994, pp. 28–34; also see Kelly Greene, "How to Survive the First Year," *The Wall Street Journal*, June 9, 2003, p. R1.

pp. 2 and 8, adjustment to retirement: Partially adapted from Gail Sheehy, *New Passages: Mapping Your Life Across Time*, New York, Ballantine Books, 1995, especially chapters 16, 17, and 19.

pp. 4–6, discussions of accomplishment, relevancy, social relationships, and direction: Partially adapted from Vern Drilling, *Closing Doors, Opening Worlds*, Minneapolis: Deaconess Press, 1993.

p. 7, story of Carl K.: Carl H. Klaus, *Taking Retirement*, Boston: Beacon Press, 1999; Lisa Reilly Cullen, "The Freshman," *Money*, July 2000, pp. 115–119.

Step 1. The Propellant:
Know the Driving Force

pp. 12–13, story of Gib J.: Jack Wyman, *Retired? Get Back in the Game!* Scottsdale, AZ: Doer Publications, 1994, p. 113.

pp. 16–17, seminars on creativity: J.A.B. McLeish, *The Ulyssean Adult: Creativity in the Middle and Later Years*, Toronto: McGraw-Hill Ryerson, 1976.

p. 17, resiliency of the brain: University of Toronto, "Old Brains Can Learn New Tricks: Study Shows Older People Use Different Areas of the Brain to Perform Same 'Thinking Task' as Young," *Science Daily*, October 25, 1999.

p. 17, comprehension and memory: Donald H. Kausler and Barry C. Kausler, *The Graying of America: An Encyclopedia of Aging, Health, Mind and Behavior*, 2nd Edition, Champaign, IL: University of Illinois Press, 2001.

p. 17, rewiring of the brain: Jeffery M. Schwartz, M.D., and Sharon Begley, *The Mind and the Brain: Neuroplasticity and the Power of Mental Force*, ReganBooks, a division of HarperCollins Publishers, 2002, as reported by Sharon Begley, "Survival of the Busiest," *The Wall Street Journal*, Friday, October 11, 2002, p. B1.

p. 17, chronological age is unreliable: Leonard Hayflick, *How and Why We Age*, New York: Ballantine, 1994.

pp. 17–19, stories of the four nonagenarians: Ron Hoffman, "Working Past 90," *Fortune*, November 13, 2000, pp. 364–384.

p. 18, story of Robert E.: CNN *Moneyline*, November 6, 2000.

p. 19, you're not alone: AARP Research Center, "Staying Ahead of the Curve: The AARP Work and Career Study, *AARP*, September, 2002.

p. 19, as reported in the Journal of Gerontology: Barbara McIntosh and Nick Danigelis, "The Complicated Fit Between Productive Activity for Elders Affect," *Journal of Gerontology: Social Sciences*, March 1995.

pp. 19–20, study of physicians: Kausler and Kausler, 2001.

p. 20, results of young animal studies: Reported by Gail Sheehy, *Understanding Men's Passages*, New York: Ballantine Books, 1999, p. 258.

p. 20, one researcher, Scott Rex: "Language and Longevity," <linguistics.ucdavis.edu/Linghp38.html>, 2002.

p. 20, story of trapped miners: Deepak Chopra, *Unconditional Life: Discovering the Power to Fulfill Your Dreams*, New York: Bantam Books, 1991.

p. 21, Duke University study: Reported by Valerie Young, <www.ChangingCourse.com>, September 9, 2002.

p. 21, longevity: Deepak Chopra, *Ageless Body, Timeless Mind: The Quantum Alternative to Growing Old*, New York: Crown Publishing Group, 1993, p. 100; Sherwin B. Nuland, *How We Die: Reflections on Life's Final Chapter*, New York: Knopf, 1994, and *The Wisdom of the Body*, New York: Knopf, 1997, p. 28 (both sources reported in Helen Harkness, *Don't Stop the Career Clock*, Palo Alto, CA: Davies-Black Publishing, 1999).

p. 21, retirement may shorten your life: Denis Waitley, *The Winners Edge*, Chicago: Nightingale-Conant Corporation (audio tape).

p. 22, put setbacks in better perspective: Gene Cohen, *The Creative Age: Awakening Human Potential in the Second Half of Life*, HarperCollins Publishers, 2001.

Step 2. The Clues: Learn from the Successes and Failures of Others

pp. 29–30, changing occupations and/or industries: Adapted from Richard Nelson Bolles, *What Color Is Your Parachute?* Berkeley, CA: Ten Speed Press, 2003, pp. 8–10. Check this source for a more detailed description.

pp. 31–32, story of Gib J.: Wyman, 1994.

p. 37, story of Bobby P.: Cullen, p. 119.

Step 3. The Target: Zero in on the Object of Your Search

pp. 39–40, "musts" and "wants": Charles H. Kepner and Benjamin B. Tregoe, *The Rational Manager*, New York: McGraw-Hill, 1965, pp. 183-184.

pp. 40–41, story of Humberto C.: Humberto Cruz, syndicated columnist for Tribune Media Services, "Retirement Years for Many Will Still Include Working," as published in *The Arizona Republic*, 2001.

p. 57, story of Don D.: Web site, 2Young2Retire, 2002.

Step 4. The Paths: Explore Alternative Ways to Your Renaissance

p. 66, story of Gib J.: Wyman, 1994.

p. 67, definitions: These are adapted from those found in Bolles, 2003, pp. 8–10.

pp. 68–69, story of Carl K.: Cullen, 2000.

pp. 69–71, 73, story of Walter W.: Hoffman, 2000; and personal interview, 2002.

pp. 106–109, story of John "Jack" A.: Wyman, 1994, pp. 126–131.

pp. 110–111, story of Harold A.: Marc Freedman, "The New Unretirement," Modern Maturity, January–February, 2001, p. 56.

pp. 110, 114–115, 120, story of Mark B.: Robert K. Otterbourg, Retire & Thrive, Washington, D.C.: Kiplinger Books, 1999, pp. 117–118.

p. 115, story of Al F.: Web site, 2Young2Retire, 2002.

pp. 117–118, 120, story of Dr. Bill S.: Freedman, 2001, pp. 54, 56.

pp. 118, 120, story of Bobby P.: Cullen, 2000, p. 119.

pp. 119, 120, story of Herbert "Herb" H.: Otterbourg, 1999, pp. 111–112.

Step 5. The Plan: Make Your Renaissance a Reality

p. 124, Dr. Walter W.: Hoffman, 2002.

p. 126, study of lucky people: Max Gunther, The Luck Factor, New York: Macmillan, 1977, pp. 168–181.

p. 127, Don D.: 2Young2Retire, 2002.

p. 134, Humberto C.: The Arizona Republic, 2001.

Appendix A. Research Resources

p. 147, Jack A.: Wyman, 2002.

p. 151, putting your resume on a job site and not expecting miraculous results: Bolles, 2003, pp. 20–28, 32.

p. 158, course for "unretirement": North Carolina Center for Creative Retirement, <rocky.unca.edu/ncccr/>.

pp. 160–161, using career counselors: Sarah Breckenridge, "Wired for Hire," SmartMoney, March 2001, p. 105, and Bolles, 2003, pp. 393–404.

About the Author

Dr. Robert E. Linneman is the founder of Renaissance Counselors. Formerly he was a marketing professor at Temple and Saint Joseph's universities. While at Temple University, he was a recipient of the Lindback Award for distinguished teaching and also served as associate dean of the School of Business and dean of Temple University Japan. As a professor and administrator, he has been involved in counseling students and professionals for almost 40 years.

He has also worked in industrial sales and has served as director of marketing for a major corporation. As a consultant, he has participated in marketing and planning projects for over 60 companies.

Dr. Linneman is the author or co-author of more than 50 articles in professional journals, including the *Harvard Business Review* and Massachusetts Institute of Technology's *Sloan Management Review*. He has also authored or co-authored four books, two of which have been translated into a number of foreign languages.

A frequent speaker, he has given seminars and speeches nationally and in Canada, Central and South America, Asia, Africa, and Europe.

Dr. Linneman is also active in professional and community organizations. He has served, for example, as vice president and director for the American Marketing Association and is currently a mentor and board member for Chester County Futures, Pennsylvania, and a member of the Philadelphia Area Coaches Alliance.

Comments to the Author

Book Update

For the sake of future editions of this book, I'd appreciate any comments or suggestions you'd care to make. I would truly be interested in hearing from you.

Personal Coaching

Interested in finding out more about personal coaching? Let me know and I'll send you a packet of information.

Wishing you the best,

Robert E. Linneman
Renaissance Counselors
155 Jug Hollow Road
Valley Forge, PA 19481

E-mail: Rlinneman@Renaissance-not-Retirement.com

Printed in the United States
21514LVS00003B/296